Italian
Word Puzzles

```
          ¹V
    ²I     O        ³E
     T     C         N
⁴G R A M M A T I C A
 I   L     B         G
 O   I     O         M
 C   A     L         I
 H   N     A         S
 I   O     R         T
           I         I
           O         C
                     A
```

Italian Word Puzzles

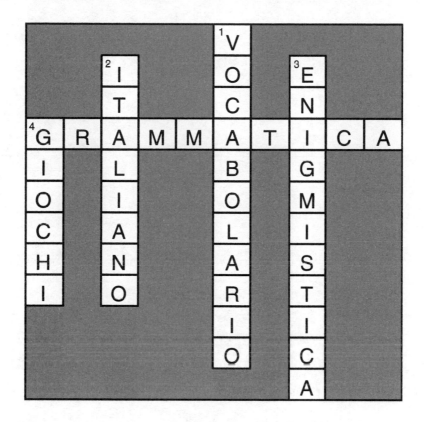

Marcel Danesi, Ph.D.

University of Toronto

BARRON'S

All inquiries should be addressed to:
Barron's Educational Series, Inc.
250 Wireless Boulevard
Hauppauge, New York 11788
http://www.barronseduc.com

ISBN-13: 978-0-7641-3322-0
ISBN-10: 0-7641-3322-5

Printed in the United States of America

9 8 7 6 5 4 3 2 1

Contents

Preface

A good puzzle is its own reward, as the saying goes! Puzzles also have a hidden educational benefit—they can help us learn subjects such as languages easily and efficiently. This book contains a collection of word puzzles designed to help the beginning or intermediate student of Italian work on the basics of vocabulary and grammar in an enjoyable and effortless way. All you need is a love for solving puzzles. If you are a beginning student, you can use this manual specifically to support and reinforce what you are studying; if you are an intermediate student, you can use this manual instead to brush up and expand your knowledge.

The puzzles cover common topics such as food, clothing, plants, verbs, and Italian culture. They come in five formats (crosswords, word crosses, scrambled letters, word searches, cryptograms) and increasing levels of difficulty—from easy to challenging. This is why they are numbered consecutively. As used here, the term "level of difficulty" means that the puzzle clues will become gradually more difficult linguistically as you progress through the book—for example, in the easy- and moderate-level sections you will find that most of the clues are pictures or English equivalents, whereas in the tough and challenging sections you will find more and more clues that are given only in the Italian language. It means, additionally, that the solution involves knowing uncommon or unusual vocabulary (names of trees, animals, etc.) or more technical matters.

No matter at what stage of linguistic knowledge you find yourself, you are bound to hit upon specific puzzles that you can solve easily, given the large selection provided—100 in total! The best thing, however, is to try doing them all, starting at the beginning and working your way right through to the most challenging ones. At the end of the book, you will find the answers to all the puzzles and a handy "word finder," which lists the words and expressions that you will need to solve the puzzles. Even if you cannot solve some particular puzzle, you will gain linguistically just the same by simply reading its solution. The purpose of this book is, after all, to help you gain proficiency in the Italian language, not just in puzzle-solving. So, do not leave any puzzle half done or completely undone. Try your best to solve each and every one in its entirety. However, if you do get bogged down, look up the answer and finish the puzzle by simply copying the answer. This will ensure that you have gained something useful from it.

The emphasis throughout the book is on vocabulary development. Three grammar word search sections have been thrown in for good measure (at the moderate, tough, and challenging levels). To help you solve these there is a *Grammar Charts* section at the back, which you can consult, especially if you need to brush up on some particular point of grammar.

Italian Word Puzzles will bring you hours and hours of learning fun, especially if you already know a little Italian. All you need is a tad of patience and a knack for solving puzzles.

Marcel Danesi
Toronto, 2006

Easy Puzzles

The puzzles in this part are classified as "easy" because the clues given are of the simple variety: pictures and English equivalents. Also, you are given many hints, many more than in any of the remaining parts. And throughout this part you are given the article form that precedes a noun. Have fun!

CROSSWORDS

The House (La casa)

1. **Rooms** (Stanze)

   In this puzzle, the clues are all equivalent English terms referring to rooms, parts of rooms, and so on (kitchen, door, ceiling…).

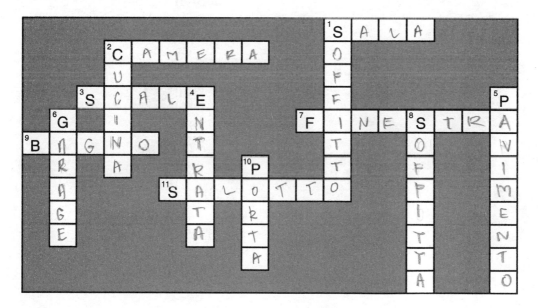

Across	Down
1. dining room (la … da pranzo)	1. ceiling (il …)
2. bedroom (la … da letto)	2. kitchen (la …)
3. stairs (le …)	4. entrance (l'…)
7. window (la …)	5. floor (il …)
9. bathroom (il …)	6. garage (il …)
11. living room (il …)	8. attic (la …)
	10. door (la …)

1

2. At Table (A tavola)

The clues are either pictures or equivalent English terms referring to the kinds of things found at table. The required word refers to the container represented by the picture, not its contents (plate, bottle, cup...).

Across

2. tablecloth (la ...)
4. (il ...)

6. (la ...)

8. to drink
9. (la ...)

11. spoon (il ...)
12. to serve
13. fork (la ...)

Down

1. to eat
3. (la ...)

5. knife (il ...)
7. (il ...)

10. (la ...)

3. Furniture (La mobilia)

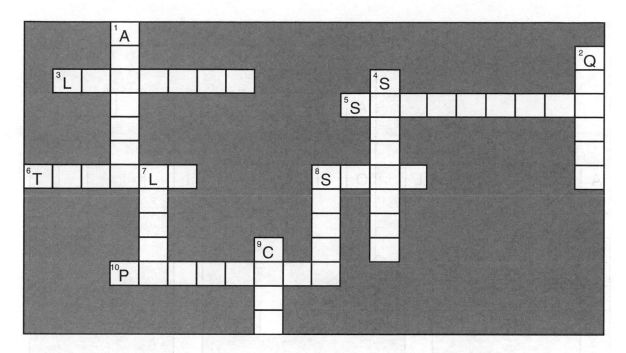

Across

3. lamp (la ...)
5. (la ...)

6. table (la ...)
8. (il ...)

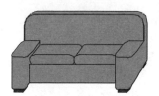

10. (la ...)

Down

1. cabinet (l'...)
2. painting (il ...)
4. (lo ...)

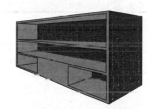

7. (il ...)

8. (la ...)

9. dresser (il ...)

4. Objects, Appliances, and Fixtures (Oggetti, elettrodomestici e impianti)

Across

2. (la ...)

3. (l'...)

Down

1. (la ...)

4. (la ...)

Across (continued)

7. (l'...)

9. (il ...)

10. (gli ...)

Down (continued)

5. (l'...)

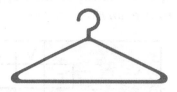

6. (la ...)

8. (l'...)

5. Recreation at Home (Il relax a casa)

The clues are, once again, pictures of familiar household things used for recreation (compact disc, radio, and so on).

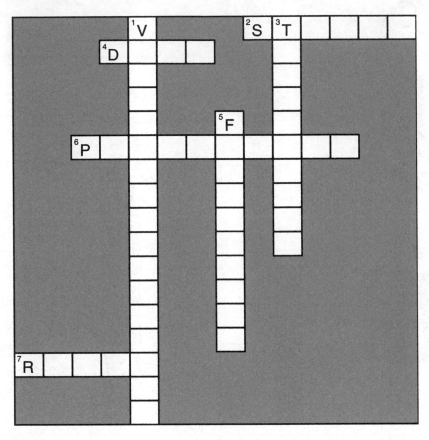

Across

2. (lo ...)

4. (il compact ...)

6. (l'antenna ...)

7. (la ...)

Down

1. (il ...)

3. (il ...)

5. (la ...)

WORD CROSSES

Family and People (La famiglia e la gente)

The given word in the vertical column of each puzzle is related to the theme of the puzzle.

6.   The Family (La famiglia)

The clues are equivalent English kinship terms.

1	M
2	A
3	T
4	E
5	R
6	N
7	I
8	T
9	À

Clues

1. mother (la ...)
2. aunt (la ...)
3. brother (il ...)
4. sister (la ...)
5. father (il ...)
6. grandparents (i ...)
7. uncle (lo ...)
8. little cousins (i ...)
9. dad (il ...)

7. People (La gente)

The clues are, again, equivalent English terms referring to people this time.

Clues

1. populace (il ...)

2. girls (le ...)

3. boys (i ...)

4. human being (l'... umano)

5. man (l'...)

6. woman (la ...)

7. people (la ...)

8. The Body (Il corpo)

```
  1 [ ][A][ ][ ]
  2    [N][ ][ ][ ]
3 [ ][ ][A][ ][ ][ ]
  4    [T][ ][ ][ ][ ]
  5    [O][ ][ ][ ][ ][ ][ ]
6 [ ][ ][M][ ][ ]
  7   [ ][I][ ][ ]
8 [ ][ ][C][ ][ ]
  9  [ ][O][ ][ ][ ]
```

Clues

1. (la ...)

2. (il ...)

3. (il ...)

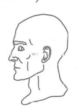

4. (la ...)

5. (l'...)

6. (la ...)

7. (il ...)

8. (l'...)

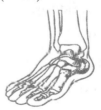

9. (la ...)

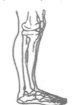

9. Physique (L'apparenza fisica)

The clues are equivalent English terms referring to physical traits (tall, short...).

Clues

1. thin, skinny
2. bony
3. fat
4. slender
5. huge
6. athletic
7. tall
8. short
9. strong

10. Personality (La personalità)

The clues are equivalent English terms referring to personality traits (nice, kind...).

Clues

1. creative
2. nice
3. generous
4. calm
5. quiet
6. gentle, kind
7. sincere
8. rough, uncouth
9. nervous

SCRAMBLED LETTERS
Basic Notions (Nozioni di base)

The first column contains the scrambled letters of the word or expression to which the clue in the middle column applies. Write the answer in the third column by unscrambling the letters.

11. Numbers (I numeri)

Each clue is a number. Can you figure out its verbal equivalent? As a hint, you are given the first letter of each answer.

Scrambled Letters	Clues	Answers
1. DDIOCI	12	D _____
2. STTAENTA	70	S _____
3. OTANTTA	80	O _____
4. CENTRETO	300	T _____
5. NU TRZOE	1/3	U _____
6. LLMIE	1 000	M _____
7. NU MIONILE	1 000 000	U _____
8. IMPRO	1st	P _____
9. QCESIMUINDIO	15th	Q _____
10. VNESIENTUMO	21st	V _____

12. Time (Le ore)

Each clue is a number indicating time of day. What is the verbal equivalent of the number?
As a hint, you are given the first letter of each answer.

Scrambled Letters	Clues	Answers
1. MZZOGIEORNO	12:00 P.M.	M _____
2. MZANOTEZTE	12:00 A.M.	M _____
3. L'NUA E CNQIUE	1:05	L' _____
4. L'NUA E MEOZZ	1:30	L' _____
5. EL UED E NU QRTUAO	2:15	L _____
6. EL DECII EDL MTTAINO	10 A.M.	L _____
7. EL VNTIEDUE	10 P.M.	L _____
8. EL TORQUATDICI	2:00 P.M.	L _____

13. The Weather (Il tempo)

Scrambled Letters	Clues	Answers

1. NLOSUVOO

È …

_____

2. PERCOTO

Il cielo è …

_____

3. ESOL

C'è il …

_____

4. VTOEN

Tira …

_____

5. FDDREO

Fa …

_____

6. CDOAL

Fa …

_____

7. PVIOE

... a dirotto

8. NVEICA

... spesso in inverno

_____

_____

14. Colors (Colori)

Scrambled Letters	Clues	Answers
1. RSSOO	red	R _____
2. URRAZZO	blue	A _____
3. VRDEE	green	V _____
4. ALLGIO	yellow	G _____
5. MARONRE	brown	M _____
6. VLAIO	purple	V _____
7. RSAO	pink	R _____
8. NCBIAO	white	B _____
9. NROE	black	N _____
10. ACIONRANE	orange	A _____

15. Qualities (Qualità)

The clues are equivalent English terms referring to qualities of things (round, smooth...).
As a hint, you are given the first letter of each answer.

Scrambled Letters	Clues	Answers
1. LCDOE	sweet	D _____
2. AARMO	bitter	A _____
3. DROU	hard	D _____
4. MLLOE	soft	M _____
5. RONDOTO	round	R _____
6. LCIISO	smooth	L _____
7. OULATNDO	wavy	O _____
8. BNATAGO	wet	B _____
9. AUTTSCIO	dry	A _____

WORD SEARCHES
Clothing and Footwear
(Abbigliamento e calzature)

The hidden words can be read in one of three directions:
from left to right, from right to left, and top down.
Circle them.

16. Clothing (L'abbigliamento)

*The clues are equivalent English terms referring to clothes. As a hint, you are given the
number of letters in each hidden word.*

Q	A	P	E	R	T	U	I	O	P	L	G	A
S	C	A	P	P	E	L	L	O	D	T	I	I
Z	C	N	E	R	T	U	I	O	P	L	A	S
Q	P	T	S	C	D	F	G	H	L	O	C	O
C	R	A	V	A	T	T	A	R	T	U	C	O
T	T	L	I	M	T	U	I	O	P	L	A	L
O	O	O	O	I	O	V	O	M	C	A	D	S
P	P	N	P	C	P	E	P	A	C	A	D	S
M	M	I	M	I	M	S	M	G	O	N	N	A
N	N	P	N	A	N	T	N	L	C	A	D	S
B	B	M	B	S	B	I	B	I	C	A	D	S
C	A	M	I	C	E	T	T	A	C	A	D	S
A	S	D	G	C	O	O	I	L	O	P	T	V

Clues

1. pants, trousers (letters = 9) (i ...)
2. hat (letters = 8) (il ...)
3. tie (letters = 8) (la ...)
4. jacket (letters = 6) (la ...)
5. shirt (letters = 7) (la ...)

6. blouse (letters = 9) (la ...)
7. skirt (letters = 5) (la ...)
8. dress (letters = 7) (il ...)
9. sweater (letters = 6) (la ...)

17. Footwear (Le calzature)

```
Q  E  R  T  A  S  U  O  L  A  C  U  S
Q  E  R  T  A  T  G  H  U  I  O  P  A
A  C  A  L  Z  I  N  O  L  O  D  C  N
S  A  L  O  D  V  H  U  I  O  P  D
D  L  U  I  O  A  G  H  U  I  O  P  A
F  Z  U  I  O  L  G  H  U  I  O  P  L
G  A  U  I  O  E  B  N  T  A  C  C  O
H  A  S  D  R  E  T  U  I  O  P  L  I
L  A  S  A  P  R  A  C  S  D  C  U  I
```

Clues

1. boot (letters = 7) (lo ...)
2. sock (letters = 7) (il ...)
3. shoe (letters = 6) (la ...)
4. stocking (letters = 5) (la ...)
5. sandal (letters = 7) (il ...)
6. heel (letters = 5) (il ...)
7. sole (letters = 5) (la ...)

18. Jewelry (I gioielli)

```
A   N   E   L   L   O   A   R   D   G   N   M   O
V   C   U   I   O   R   B   N   M   G   C   H   U
C   D   A   S   C   O   L   L   A   N   A   T   R
P   S   R   T   I   L   C   D   A   S   T   H   U
V   C   U   I   O   O   C   D   A   S   E   M   O
P   S   R   T   I   G   C   D   A   S   N   T   R
R   D   G   S   P   I   L   L   A   Q   A   H   U
V   C   U   I   O   O   V   C   U   I   O   T   R
P   S   R   T   I   V   C   U   I   O   P   M   O
O   R   E   C   C   H   I   N   O   T   R   H   U
```

Clues

1. watch (letters = 8) (l'...)
2. ring (letters = 6) (l'...)
3. necklace (letters = 7) (la ...)
4. chain (letters = 6) (la ...)
5. earring (letters = 9) (l'...)
6. broach (letters = 6) (la ...)

19. Accessories and Things (Accessori e cose varie)

```
S   C   C   C   G   C   G   C   C   C   A   G   H
C   A   I   A   B   A   U   A   A   A   B   I   I
I   D   N   D   O   D   A   D   D   D   O   O   O
A   S   T   S   R   S   N   S   S   S   T   P   P
R   D   U   D   S   D   T   D   D   D   T   L   L
P   O   R   T   A   F   O   G   L   I   O   H   H
A   S   A   C   A   D   S   D   M   L   N   N   N
C   A   D   S   D   M   L   G   H   I   E   M   M
C   A   D   S   D   M   L   G   M   I   L   E   E
```

Clues

1. purse (letters = 5) (la ...)
2. glove (letters = 6) (il ...)
3. scarf (letters = 7) (la ...)
4. belt (letters = 7) (la ...)
5. button (letters = 7) (il ...)
6. wallet (letters = 11) (il ...)

20. Getting Dressed (Vestirsi)

The clues are, again, equivalent English terms referring to dressing. You are also given the number of letters in each hidden word.

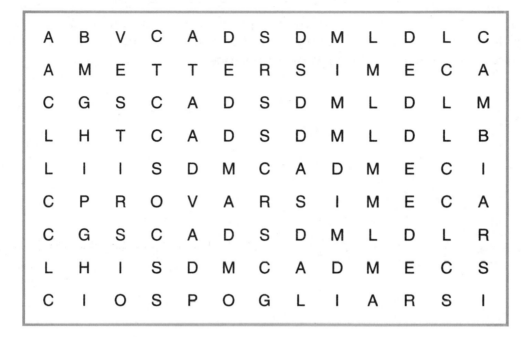

```
A  B  V  C  A  D  S  D  M  L  D  L  C
A  M  E  T  T  E  R  S  I  M  E  C  A
C  G  S  C  A  D  S  D  M  L  D  L  M
L  H  T  C  A  D  S  D  M  L  D  L  B
L  I  I  S  D  M  C  A  D  M  E  C  I
C  P  R  O  V  A  R  S  I  M  E  C  A
C  G  S  C  A  D  S  D  M  L  D  L  R
L  H  I  S  D  M  C  A  D  M  E  C  S
C  I  O  S  P  O  G  L  I  A  R  S  I
```

Clues

1. to get dressed (letters = 8)
2. to put on (letters = 8)
3. to change (letters = 9)
4. to get undressed (letters = 10)
5. to try on (letters = 8)

CRYPTOGRAMS
Greetings, Introductions ...
(Saluti, presentazioni ...)

A specific number will correspond to a specific letter in all the cryptograms. For example, if you establish that 1 = H in any one of the five puzzles, then you can go ahead and substitute H for each occurrence of the digit 1 in the remaining puzzles. The clues for all the puzzles are equivalent English words or expressions.

21. Greetings (Saluti)

1. Hi!

$$\frac{C}{1} \; \frac{}{2} \; \frac{}{3} \; \frac{}{4}$$

2. Good-bye!

$$\frac{}{3} \; \frac{}{5} \; \frac{}{5} \; \frac{I}{2} \; \frac{}{6} \; \frac{}{7} \; \frac{}{8} \; \frac{}{7} \; \frac{}{5} \; \frac{}{1} \; \frac{}{2}$$

22. Introductions (Presentazioni)

1. My name is ...

$$\frac{M}{9} \; \frac{}{2} \qquad \frac{}{1} \; \frac{}{11} \; \frac{}{2} \; \frac{}{3} \; \frac{}{9} \; \frac{}{4}$$

2. A pleasure!

$$\frac{P}{10} \; \frac{}{2} \; \frac{}{3} \; \frac{}{1} \; \frac{}{7} \; \frac{}{5} \; \frac{}{7}$$

23. Names (I nominativi)

1. given (first) name

$$\frac{}{12} \; \frac{}{4} \; \frac{}{9} \; \frac{}{7}$$

2. surname (family name)

$$\frac{}{1} \; \frac{}{4} \; \frac{}{13} \; \frac{}{12} \; \frac{}{4} \; \frac{}{9} \; \frac{}{7}$$

24. Addresses (Gli indirizzi)

1. street

$\overline{14}$ $\overline{15}$ $\overline{5}$ $\overline{3}$ $\overline{8}$ $\overline{3}$

2. I live at …

$\overline{3}$ $\overline{16}$ $\overline{2}$ $\overline{15}$ $\overline{4}$ $\quad$ $\overline{2}$ $\overline{12}$ $\quad$ $\overline{6}$ $\overline{2}$ $\overline{3}$

25. Phoning (Telefonare)

1. Hello!

$\overline{10}$ $\overline{5}$ $\overline{4}$ $\overline{12}$ $\overline{15}$ $\overline{4}$

2. phone number (numero …)

$\overline{15}$ $\overline{7}$ $\overline{17}$ $\overline{7}$ $\overline{18}$ $\overline{4}$ $\overline{12}$ $\overline{2}$ $\overline{1}$ $\overline{4}$

Moderate-Level Puzzles

The puzzles in this part are a bit harder than the ones in the previous part. The clues are similar. Most are, again, pictures or English equivalents. However, Italian material is used in the word cross sections. You are given plenty of hints, but fewer than in the previous part. You are again given the article form that precedes a noun. Again, have fun!

CROSSWORDS
Food (Gli alimenti)

26. Vegetables (I legumi)

Across

1. (i ...)

5. (la ...)

7. (la ...)

9. (il ...)

10. (il ...)

11. (il ...)

Down

2. (il ...)

3. (il ...)

4. (il ...)

6. (il ...)

8. (la ...)

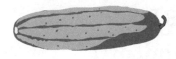

9. (le ...)

27. Fruit (La frutta)

Across

3. (la ...)

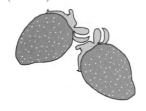

6. (i ...)

7. (le ...)

Down

1. (la ...)

2. (l'...)

4. (le ...)

Across (continued)

8. (la ...)

9. (la ...)

11. (l' ...)

Down (continued)

5. (l'...)

9. (la ...)

10. (il ...)

28. Meat and Fish (La carne e il pesce)

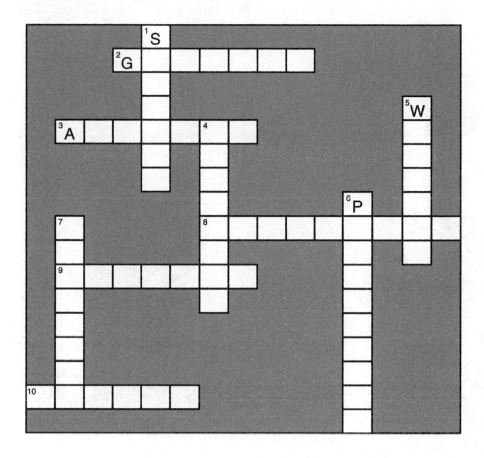

Across

2. (i ...)

3. (l'... con le patate)

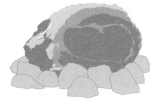

Down

1. (il ...)

4. (il ...)

Across (continued)

8. (l'...)

9. (le ...)

10. (il ...)

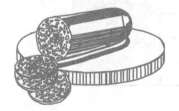

Down (continued)

5. (il ...)

6. (il ...)

7. (la ...)

29. Bread and Sweets (Il pane e i dolci)

Across

3. (i ...)

6. (la ...)

Down

1. (il ...)

2. (il ...)

Across (continued)

7. (il ...)

9. (il ...)

10. (il ...)

Down (continued)

4. (la ...)

5. (la ...)

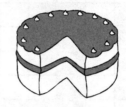

8. (i ...)

30. Other Foods and Beverages (Altri alimenti e bevande)

Across
2. (il …)

4. (le … fritte)

Down
1. (il …)

3. (gli …)

Across (continued)

6. (il ...)

7. (la ...)

8. (l'acqua ...)

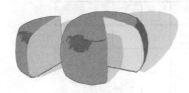

Down (continued)

5. (le ...)

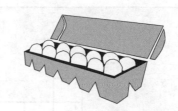

7. (il ...)

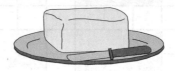

WORD CROSSES

Nouns, Adjectives, and Prepositions
(Nomi, aggettivi e preposizioni)

The given word in the vertical column of each puzzle is related to the theme of the puzzle. If you have forgotten your Italian grammar, simply consult the Grammar Charts section at the back.

31. Plural Nouns (Il plurale dei nomi)

The clues are the singular forms of the required masculine plural nouns. In Puzzle 84 you will come across feminine nouns and a few irregular nouns.

Clues

1. (il) piano
2. (il) luogo
3. (il) cuoco
4. (il) giornale
5. (l') amico
6. (il) falco
7. (il) greco

32. Adjectives (Gli aggettivi)

Each clue consists of an English equivalent adjective. Can you figure out its corresponding Italian feminine form?

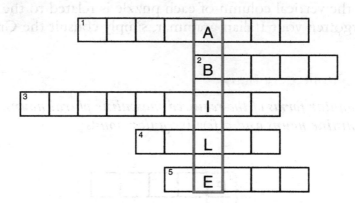

Clues

1. elegant
2. good
3. nice
4. sweet
5. beautiful

33. Demonstrative Adjectives (Gli aggettivi dimostrativi)

Can you figure out which form of the indicated demonstrative adjective (given in English) is required before each Italian word in the clues?

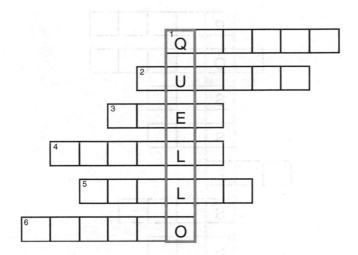

Clues

1. this ragazzo
2. these ragazze
3. those gatti
4. those amici
5. those idee
6. that studente

34. Possessive Adjectives (Gli aggettivi possessivi)

Each clue (except 1) gives you the corresponding English possessive adjective. Clue 1 is an English word for you to translate.

Clues

1. package (il ...)

2. our amiche (le ...)

3. his amico (il ...)

4. his amica (la ...)

5. my penne (le ...)

6. her amici (i ...)

7. her amiche (le ...)

8. your libri (i ...)

9. your genitori (i ...)

10. their amici (i ...)

35. Prepositions (Le preposizioni)

The clues are equivalent English prepositional phrases.

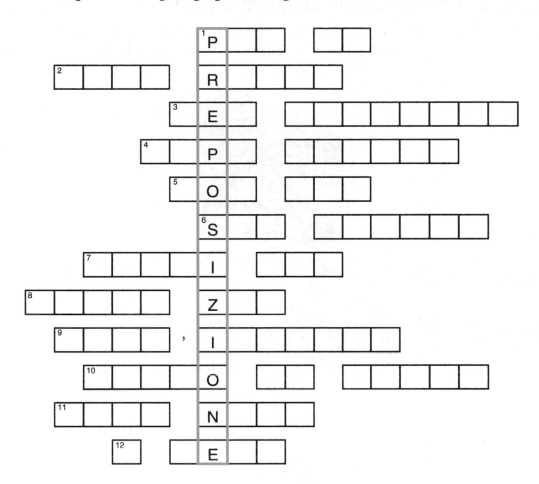

Clues

1. for me
2. on the radio
3. in the drawer
4. after tomorrow
5. with us
6. on the table
7. at our uncles' (place)
8. of the uncle
9. in the winter
10. under the chair
11. at nine (o'clock)
12. at dinner

SCRAMBLED LETTERS
Eating and Drinking (Mangiare e bere)

The first column contains the scrambled letters of the word or expression to which the clue in the middle column applies. Write the answer in the third column by unscrambling the letters.

36. Drinks (Le bevande)

Scrambled Letters	Clues	Answers
1. BREE	to drink	_____
2. QUAAC	water	(l') _____
3. TESE	thirst	(la) _____
4. ALAL SLUTAE!	To your health!	_____
5. VNOI	wine	(il) _____
6. ANDBEVA ANLCOLAICA	soft drink	(la) _____
7. LNATIMOA	lemonade (fizzy)	(la) _____
8. ACIATRANA	orangeade	(l') _____

37. At the Restaurant (Al ristorante)

Scrambled Letters	Clues	Answers
1. MUEN	description of dishes	(il) _____
2. NCIAMA	tip	(la) _____
3. CERIERAME	waiter	(il) _____
4. CERIERAMA	waitress	(la) _____
5. PATTIO	dish	(il) _____
6. PZIONORE	serving	(la) _____
7. POTAZIORENNE	reservation	(la) _____

38. Let's Eat! (Mangiamo!)

The clues are equivalent English verbs referring to actions that characterize eating.

Scrambled Letters	Clues	Answers
1. MNGIAARE	to eat	_____
2. TAREAGLI	to cut	_____
3. AGGIAASSRE	to taste	_____
4. EVARSRE	to pour	_____
5. SVIREER	to serve	_____
6. PDEREREN	to have (something)	_____
7. DRIRIGEE	to digest	_____
8. VITAROME	to vomit	_____

39. Descriptions (Descrizioni)

The clues are equivalent English adjectives that describe how food is prepared or how it tastes.

Scrambled Letters	Clues	Answers
1. SLATOA	salty	_____
2. PCANICTE	spicy	_____
3. LCDOE	sweet	_____
4. ALAL GGLIRIA	grilled	_____
5. ARSTITROO	roasted	_____
6. LA FRNOO	baked	_____
7. MURATO	ripe	_____
8. APRSO	sour	_____

40. Expressions (Espressioni)

The clues are additional equivalent English expressions referring to foods, condiments, and ways of preparing food.

Scrambled Letters	Clues	Answers
1. ENB CTTOO	well-done	_____
2. LA SGUO	with sauce	_____
3. ILATNSAA ID RSIO	rice salad	(l') _____
4. APASNTITO	appetizer, starter	(l') _____
5. FTTRUI ID ARME	seafood	(i) _____
6. ETTAPA FTTRIE	fried potatoes	(le) _____

WORD SEARCHES
Cities, Traffic, and Places (Città, traffico e luoghi)

The hidden words can be read in one of three directions: from left to right, from right to left, and top down. Circle them. In each puzzle you are shown where one of the hidden words is.

41. Cities (Città)

The clues are equivalent English terms describing cities and related concepts (suburbs, bridges...).

D	O	P	E	A	D	C	D	S	L	P	T	C
P	E	N	D	O	L	A	R	E	A	E	I	E
E	F	G	I	R	T	U	I	P	O	R	O	N
D	O	P	F	A	D	C	D	S	L	I	P	T
E	F	G	I	R	T	U	I	P	O	F	E	R
D	O	P	C	A	P	I	T	A	L	E	R	O
E	F	G	I	A	D	C	D	S	L	R	S	P
E	T	N	O	P	D	C	D	S	L	I	D	E
A	D	C	D	S	L	U	I	P	O	A	V	R

Clues

1. building (l'...)
2. bridge (il ...)
3. capital of country (la ...)
4. suburbs (la ...)
5. commuter (il/la ...)
6. downtown, city center (il ...)

42. Traffic (Traffico e circolazione)

A	S	S	B	N	M	L	O	P	P	P	L	O	P
P	R	E	C	E	D	E	N	Z	A	B	N	M
C	D	M	B	N	M	L	O	P	R	L	O	P
A	S	A	C	D	P	B	N	M	C	A	S	D
C	D	F	A	S	U	L	O	P	H	L	O	P
A	S	O	A	S	N	A	S	D	I	B	N	M
F	E	R	M	A	T	A	B	L	M	L	O	P
A	S	O	C	D	A	S	D	F	E	A	S	D
B	N	M	L	O	P	M	L	O	T	M	L	O
T	S	O	R	P	A	S	S	A	R	E	B	L
B	N	M	L	O	P	M	L	O	O	A	S	D

Clues

1. (il ...)

2. (la ...)

3. (il ...)

4. (la ...)

5. to pass
6. rush hour (l'ora di ...)

43. Roads (Circolazione)

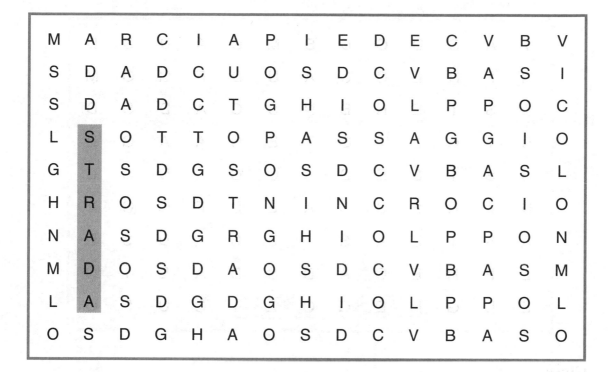

Clues

1. road (la …)
2. alley (il …)
3. intersection (l'…)
4. sidewalk (il …)
5. underpass (il …)
6. highway (l'…)

44. Buildings (Edifici)

```
T  A  S  D  C  D  S  M  C  A  D  S  D
R  F  R  E  C  C  A  U  D  F  G  O  M
I  S  I  E  H  B  N  S  C  A  D  S  D
B  I  B  L  I  O  T  E  C  A  A  G  H
U  S  I  E  E  D  S  O  C  A  D  S  D
N  F  R  E  S  C  A  E  D  F  G  O  M
A  S  I  E  A  S  I  E  C  A  D  S  D
L  F  R  E  C  A  D  S  D  A  E  I  O
E  D  G  N  E  G  O  Z  I  O  U  P  O
```

Clues
1. church (la ...)
2. museum (il ...)
3. library (la ...)
4. courthouse (il ...)
5. store (il ...)

45. Places (Luoghi)

A	G	R	T	R	C	A	D	S	D	S	A	B
S	I	C	I	I	C	A	D	S	D	S	A	B
P	A	R	C	O	T	R	E	Z	C	A	D	S
P	R	P	O	N	T	R	E	O	C	A	D	S
O	D	O	I	E	R	T	T	O	R	R	E	G
I	I	I	U	C	A	D	S	D	S	A	B	G
U	N	U	C	A	D	S	D	S	A	B	R	T
T	O	C	A	D	S	D	S	A	B	T	R	E
C	A	D	S	D	S	A	B	T	R	E	A	W

Clues

1. park (il ...)
2. garden (il ...)
3. district (il ...)
4. tower (la ...)
5. zoo (lo ...)

CRYPTOGRAMS
Politeness and Emotions (Cortesia e sentimenti)

A specific number will correspond to a specific letter in all the cryptograms. For example, if you establish that 1 = H in any one of the five puzzles, then you can go ahead and substitute H for each occurrence of the digit 1 in the remaining puzzles. The clues for all the puzzles are equivalent English expressions.

46. Courtesy (La cortesia)

1. Thank you!

$$\frac{G}{1} \ \frac{\ }{2} \ \frac{\ }{3} \ \frac{\ }{4} \ \frac{\ }{5} \ \frac{\ }{6}$$

2. You're welcome!

$$\frac{P}{7} \ \frac{\ }{2} \ \frac{\ }{6} \ \frac{\ }{1} \ \frac{\ }{8}$$

47. Politeness (La gentilezza)

1. Excuse me!

$$\frac{\ }{9} \ \frac{C}{10} \ \frac{\ }{11} \ \frac{\ }{9} \ \frac{\ }{5}$$

2. Please!

$$\frac{\ }{7} \ \frac{\ }{6} \ \frac{\ }{2} \qquad \frac{\ }{12} \ \frac{\ }{3} \ \frac{\ }{13} \ \frac{\ }{8} \ \frac{\ }{2} \ \frac{\ }{6}$$

48. Anger (La rabbia)

1. Enough!

$$\frac{\ }{14} \ \frac{\ }{3} \ \frac{\ }{9} \ \frac{\ }{15} \ \frac{\ }{3}$$

2. I don't believe it!

$$\frac{\ }{16} \ \frac{\ }{8} \ \frac{\ }{16} \qquad \frac{\ }{10} \ \frac{\ }{5} \qquad \frac{\ }{10} \ \frac{\ }{2} \ \frac{\ }{6} \ \frac{\ }{17} \ \frac{\ }{8}$$

49. Agreement and Disagreement (Essere e non essere d'accordo)

1. Certainly!

$\overline{10}$ $\overline{6}$ $\overline{2}$ $\overline{15}$ $\overline{8}$

2. Impossible!

$\overline{5}$ $\overline{18}$ $\overline{7}$ $\overline{8}$ $\overline{9}$ $\overline{9}$ $\overline{5}$ $\overline{14}$ $\overline{5}$ $\overline{19}$ $\overline{6}$

50. Other Expressions (Altre espressioni)

1. OK!

$\overline{13}$ $\overline{3}$ $\quad$ $\overline{14}$ $\overline{6}$ $\overline{16}$ $\overline{6}$

2. I wish!

$\overline{18}$ $\overline{3}$ $\overline{1}$ $\overline{3}$ $\overline{2}$ $\overline{5}$

Tough Puzzles

The puzzles in this part are harder because most of the clues you are given to solve them are in Italian. You may thus have to look certain things up in a dictionary. You are also given fewer hints. Unlike previous parts, you are not given the article forms in front of nouns.

CROSSWORDS
Jobs and Careers
(Lavori e carriere)

51. Jobs (Lavori)

Each clue consists of a sentence from which the word for a job or profession is missing (lawyer, doctor...).

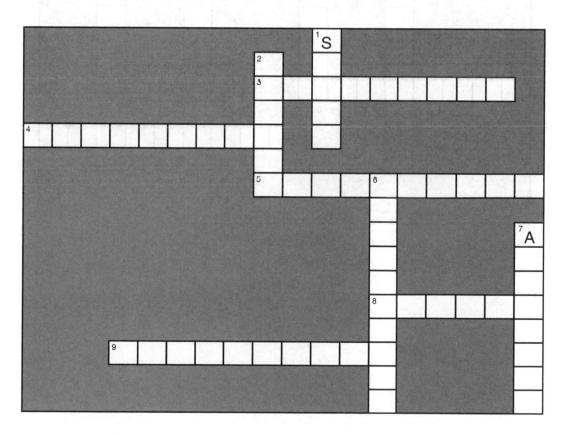

Across

3. L'... ha riparato il bagno ieri.

4. Il ... è una persona che coltiva la terra.

5. Lui è l'... che ha disegnato la nostra casa.

8. Lui è il nostro ... di famiglia.

9. Il mio amico è ... universitario.

Down

1. Quale ... ha fatto il tuo abito?

2. Mia cugina ha deciso di fare il ... d'aereo.

6. Mia sorella è ...; lavora in un ospedale vicino a casa.

7. Mio fratello è ... difensore.

52. Other Jobs (Altri lavori)

Each clue describes what the person does (as a musician, dentist...).

Across

2. suona uno strumento

4. guida l'autobus

7. taglia i capelli

8. lavora in ufficio

Down

1. lavora il legno

3. si occupa di conti

5. si occupa di impianti elettrici

6. il medico "dei denti"

53. The Office (L'ufficio)

The clues are either pictures or descriptions of office things (paper, clip, pen...).

Across

3.

4.

7. permette di unire fogli di carta (punto ...)

8.

9. strumento per scrivere

Down

1.

2.

3.

5. strumento per tagliare la carta

6. serve per cancellare

54. Workplaces (Luoghi di lavoro)

Across	Down

Luogo di occupazione di...

2. insegnanti	1. medici, infermiere...
6. camerieri	3. professori universitari
7. commessi	4. impiegati
8. contadini	5. operai

55. Working (Lavorare)

The clues are synonyms, descriptive phrases, or characterizations of concepts, activities, etc., related to working (hiring, retirement...).

Across

5. mandare via dal lavoro

6. prendere qualcuno al lavoro

7. esercitare un'attività pagata

8. Si va in ... dopo tanti anni di lavoro.

Down

1. persone senza lavoro: persone ...

2. associazione di lavoratori

3. la ... del caffè

4. lavoro

WORD CROSSES

Verbs (I verbi)

The given word in the vertical column of each puzzle is related to the theme of the puzzle. If you have forgotten your Italian verbs, simply consult the Grammar Charts section at the back.

56. The Present Indicative of Regular Verbs

(Il presente indicativo dei verbi regolari)

Each clue consists of an Italian infinitive and a pronoun. The latter indicates the present indicative form you are required to figure out. If you know your present indicative conjugations, this puzzle will turn out to be not so tough after all.

Clues

1. (parlare) tu ...
2. (vendere) lui ...
3. (dormire) lei ...
4. (finire) loro ...
5. (ricevere) voi ...

6. (amare) noi ...
7. (cantare) voi ...
8. (preferire) io ...
9. (vedere) loro ...
10. (dormire) loro ...

57. Regular and Irregular Past Participles (Participi passati regolari e irregolari)

Each clue consists of the verb in its infinitive form.

Clues

1. parlare
2. avere
3. prendere
4. essere
5. scrivere
6. capire
7. mangiare
8. sapere
9. finire

58. The Imperfect Indicative of Regular and Irregular Verbs
(L'imperfetto dei verbi regolari e irregolari)

Each clue consists of an Italian infinitive and a pronoun. The latter indicates the imperfect indicative form you are required to figure out.

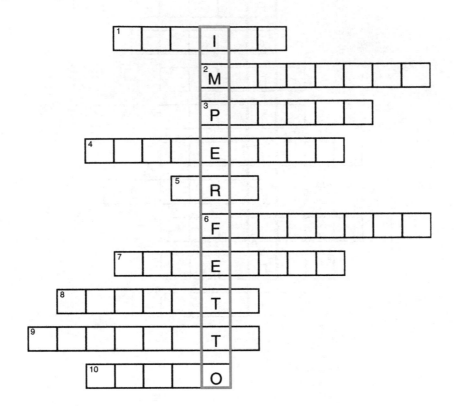

Clues
1. (finire) io ...

2. (mangiare) lei ...

3. (potere) lui ...

4. (vendere) loro ...

5. (essere) tu ...

6. (fare) noi ...

7. (dire) voi ...

8. (avere) voi ...

9. (bere) voi ...

10. (essere) loro ...

59. The Future of Regular Verbs (Il futuro dei verbi regolari)

Each clue consists of an Italian infinitive and a pronoun. The latter indicates the future form you are required to figure out.

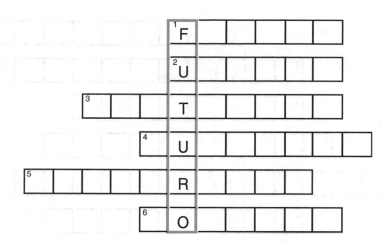

Clues

1. (finire) io ...

2. (usare) tu ...

3. (portare) noi ...

4. (guardare) lui ...

5. (vendere) loro ...

6. (dormire) io ...

60. The Conditional of Regular Verbs (Il condizionale dei verbi regolari)

Each clue consists of an Italian infinitive and a pronoun. The latter indicates the conditional form you are required to figure out. As with the previous puzzles in this section, if you know your conditional conjugations, this puzzle should be easy to solve.

Clues

1. (comprare) io ...

2. (provare) tu ...

3. (mangiare) io ...

4. (vendere) noi ...

5. (preferire) loro ...

6. (alzare) tu ...

7. (finire) io ...

8. (portare) lei

9. (cominciare) lui ...

10. (partire) voi ...

SCRAMBLED LETTERS
Recreation and Sports (Divertimenti e sport)

The first column contains the scrambled letters of the word or expression to which the clue in the middle column applies. Write the answer in the third column by unscrambling the letters.

61. Sports (Gli sport)

Each clue contains information about the sport.

Scrambled Letters	Clues	Answers
1. BSEBAALL	lo sport dei *Chicago Cubs*	_____
2. FTBAOOLL CANAMERIO	lo sport dei *Green Bay Packers*	_____
3. PACANALLESTRO	lo sport dei *Milwaukee Bucks*	_____
4. TNNEIS	lo sport delle sorelle Williams	_____
5. HCKEOY	lo sport di Wayne Gretzky	_____
6. CLCIAO	lo sport più popolare in Italia	_____
7. GLFO	lo sport di Tiger Woods	_____
8. NASTGINICA	uno sport che si pratica in palestra	_____
9. ISC	uno sport che si pratica sulla neve	_____

62. Buildings and Arenas (Edifici, stadi...)

Scrambled Letters	Clues	Answers
1. ACCIGHIO	dove ha luogo una partita di hockey	_____
2. SADITO	dove ha luogo una partita di calcio	_____
3. CMPAO	dove ha luogo una partita di football, baseball...	_____
4. PESTALRA	dove si fa la ginnastica	_____
5. PSTIA	dove si fanno le gare di sci	_____

63. Amusement (Distrarsi giocando)

Scrambled Letters	Clues	Answers
1. MDAA	gioco con dodici pedine bianche e dodici pedine nere	_____
2. SCCCAHI	la mossa vincente di questo gioco si chiama "lo scacco matto"	_____
3. RTCAE AD GCOIO	carte aventi come semi i bastoni, le spade, i denari e le coppe	_____
4. POLARE CCIAROTE	gioco che si chiama anche "cruciverba"	_____
5. PZZULE	gioco consistente di tasselli che devono essere uniti per ricostruire un'immagine	_____

64. Leisure Time (Tempo libero)

Each clue either describes the type of activity that one can engage in to enjoy leisure time (shopping, going to the movies...) or where it can take place.

Scrambled Letters	Clues	Answers
1. FREA ELDLE SESPE	attività che può svolgersi in un centro di vendita	_____
2. AARNDE LA CNEMAI	attività che coinvolge sedersi e guardare uno schermo	_____
3. PAATESSMPO	attività piacevole con cui si trascorre il tempo libero	_____
4. LTTUERA	leggere come attività abituale	_____
5. ARFE ANU PASEGGSIATA	camminata fatta per passatempo	_____
6. NTARUOE	attività che si svolge in una piscina	_____

65. Recreation (La ricreazione)

Each clue describes what the recreational activity involves (vacationing, holidays...).

Scrambled Letters	Clues	Answers
1. CAGGIMPEO	le vacanze in campagna	_____
2. NZVACAE	un periodo di libertà dal lavoro	_____
3. ECITARSERSI	allenarsi	_____
4. PTICARRAE LGI SORPT	giocare a calcio, a tennis ...	_____
5. FREA LI JOGINGG	corsa a scopo di esercizio fisico	_____

WORD SEARCHES
Health and Emergencies (Salute, urgenze varie...)

The hidden words can be read in one of three directions: from left to right, from right to left, and top down. Circle them.

66. At the Hospital (In ospedale)

S	A	D	G	H	L	O	I	M	N	O	P	G	A
O	P	E	R	A	Z	I	O	N	E	M	N	O	M
C	M	N	O	G	H	L	A	D	G	M	N	O	B
C	A	D	G	H	L	O	I	M	N	O	P	G	U
O	M	N	O	G	H	L	A	D	G	M	N	O	L
R	I	A	N	I	M	A	Z	I	O	N	E	U	A
S	A	D	G	H	L	O	I	M	N	O	P	G	N
O	B	M	A	T	E	R	N	I	T	À	G	I	Z
P	A	D	G	H	L	O	I	M	N	O	P	G	A

Clues

1. sala dove sono assistiti gli ammalati gravi

2. intervento chirurgico

3. reparto riservato alle donne incinta

4. veicolo che trasporta i feriti o gli ammalati all'ospedale

5. dove i malati e i feriti trovano immediata assistenza medica (pronto ...)

67. At the Doctor's (Dal medico)

The clues are synonyms or descriptions of physical states or problems (headache, pain...).

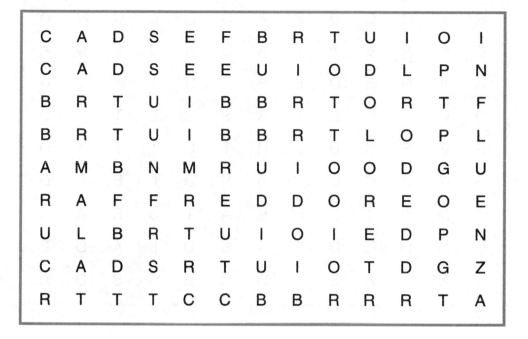

C	A	D	S	E	F	B	R	T	U	I	O	I
C	A	D	S	E	E	U	I	O	D	L	P	N
B	R	T	U	I	B	B	R	T	O	R	T	F
B	R	T	U	I	B	B	R	T	L	O	P	L
A	M	B	N	M	R	U	I	O	O	D	G	U
R	A	F	F	R	E	D	D	O	R	E	O	E
U	L	B	R	T	U	I	O	I	E	D	P	N
C	A	D	S	R	T	U	I	O	T	D	G	Z
R	T	T	T	C	C	B	B	R	R	R	T	A

Clues

1. aumento della temperatura del corpo

2. sofferenza

3. dolore alla testa (... di testa)

4. infiammazione delle vie respiratorie

5. malattia respiratoria virale molto contagiosa

68. At the Dentist's (Dal dentista)

```
R  T  C  C  D  S  A  S  D  L  D  M  D
E  C  A  V  I  T  À  E  A  U  E  U  A
A  A  R  S  D  L  R  T  U  I  N  I  U
U  U  I  C  D  S  A  S  D  L  T  L  D
B  B  E  S  D  L  R  T  U  I  I  I  O
G  G  D  C  D  S  A  S  D  L  E  L  D
I  M  P  I  O  M  B  A  T  U  R  A  P
G  G  D  C  D  S  A  S  D  L  A  D  F
I  N  I  E  Z  I  O  N  E  A  S  D  L
```

Clues

1. parte vuota all'interno di un dente
2. otturazione di un dente ammalato
3. malattia dei denti
4. si chiama anche "puntura"
5. apparecchio che sostituisce la dentatura

69. Ailments and Symptoms (Malanni e sintomi)

```
S   T   A   R   N   U   T   I   R   E   H   H   A
S   D   A   C   S   D   M   L   E   P   O   B   L
S   D   A   C   S   D   M   L   E   P   O   B   L
G   I   R   A   M   E   N   T   O   C   S   D   E
S   D   A   C   S   D   A   S   D   A   C   S   R
C   S   D   M   L   E   U   M   L   E   P   O   G
S   D   A   C   S   D   S   M   L   E   P   O   I
T   O   S   S   I   R   E   S   D   A   C   S   A
Q   R   T   U   I   O   A   B   H   I   T   G   M
```

Clues

1. avere la tosse
2. impressione di movimento circolare
3. mal di stomaco
4. avversione a particolari sostanze
5. fare starnuti

70. Emergencies (Casi di urgenze varie)

The clues are synonyms or descriptions of people involved in emergency situations (thief, police...).

A	U	S	I	L	I	A	R	E	A	D	R	P
C	A	D	S	D	S	M	L	L	E	D	A	O
A	G	G	R	E	S	S	O	R	E	E	R	M
C	A	D	S	D	S	M	L	L	E	D	A	P
A	L	C	A	D	S	D	S	M	L	L	E	I
D	A	D	S	D	S	M	L	L	E	D	A	E
T	D	D	S	D	S	M	L	L	E	D	A	R
E	R	D	S	D	S	M	L	L	E	D	A	E
P	O	L	I	Z	I	O	T	T	O	D	T	H

Clues

1. chi ruba

2. membro del corpo di polizia

3. vigile del fuoco

4. assisente medico (... medico)

5. chi aggredisce

CRYPTOGRAMS
Appearance, Mood, and Intelligence
(Apparenza fisica, umore e intelligenza)

A specific number will correspond to a specific letter in all the cryptograms. For example, if you establish that 1 = H in any one of the five puzzles, then you can go ahead and substitute H for each occurrence of the digit 1 in the remaining puzzles. The clues for the puzzles are synonyms, near synonyms, or descriptions.

71. Hair (I capelli)

1. accorciarsi la lunghezza dei capelli: ... i capelli

   T _ _ _ _ _ _ _
   1 2 3 4 5 2 6 13

2. Chi taglia i capelli alle donne.

   _ A _ _ _ _ _ _ _ _ _ _
   8 2 6 6 9 10 10 11 5 13 6 13

72. Cosmetics (I prodotti di bellezza)

1. Si applica sulle unghie.

   _ _ _ _ _ _
   7 14 2 4 1 15

2. Si applica sul viso.

   _ _ _ _ _ _
   1 6 9 10 10 15

73. Mood (L'umore)

1. felicità

   _ _ _ _ _
   3 5 15 5 2

2. infelicità

   _ _ _ _ _ _ _ _ _
   1 6 5 7 1 13 16 16 2

74. Intelligence (L'intelligenza)

1. creatività

$$\overline{17} \; \overline{2} \; \overline{18} \; \overline{1} \; \overline{2} \; \overline{7} \; \overline{5} \; \overline{2}$$

2. sciocchezza

$$\overline{7} \; \overline{1} \; \overline{9} \; \overline{8} \; \overline{5} \; \overline{19} \; \overline{5} \; \overline{1} \; \overline{2}$$

75. Character (Il carattere)

1. persona che persegue il
    proprio benessere

$$\overline{13} \; \overline{3} \; \overline{15} \; \overline{5} \; \overline{7} \; \overline{1} \; \overline{2}$$

2. persona che persegue il
    benessere degli altri

$$\overline{2} \; \overline{4} \; \overline{1} \; \overline{6} \; \overline{9} \; \overline{5} \; \overline{7} \; \overline{1} \; \overline{2}$$

Challenging Puzzles

The puzzles in this part are the hardest in this book, but certainly not impossible to do. The clues require a little more effort and, maybe, looking things up in a dictionary. You are not given any hints whatsoever. You are on your own. As always, have fun!

CROSSWORDS
Flora and Fauna
(La flora e la fauna)

76. Plants (Piante)

The clues are descriptions, illustrations, etc. of types of plants, components of plants, etc. (flowers, roots ...).

Across	Down
2. una rosa, un tulipano …	1. erba selvatica
4. parte che nasce dal fusto di un albero	3. è generalmente verde
7. pianta con fusto di legno	5. fusto
8. componente sotterranea di una pianta	6. semi

77. Animals (Animali)

Do you recognize the following animals? Can you name them in Italian? Unless you are an animal lover, this is truly a challenging puzzle. Good luck!

Across

3.

7.

Down

1.

2.

Across (continued)

9.

11.

12.

13.

15.

16.

Down (continued)

4.

5.

6.

8.

10.

14.

78. Birds (Uccelli)

Do you recognize the following birds? Can you name them in Italian?

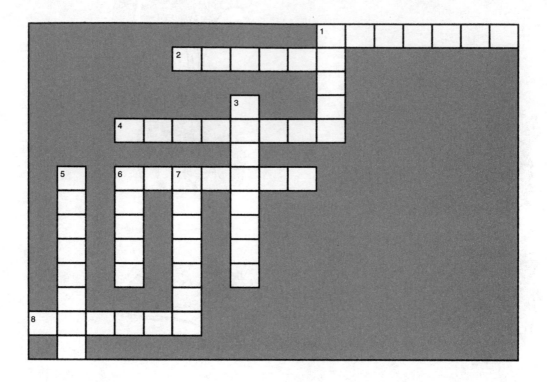

Across

1.

2.

Down

1.

3.

Across (continued)

4.

6.

8.

Down (continued)

5.

6.

7.

79. Trees (Alberi)

Across

3. l'albero che produce castagne
5. l'albero che produce le mele
6. l'albero di Natale
7. l'albero che produce le pere

Down

1. l'albero che produce le ghiande
2. l'albero che produce le olive
3. l'albero che produce le ciliege
4. l'albero la cui foglia si trova come simbolo sulla bandiera canadese

80. Flowers (Fiori)

Across

2.

6.

Down

1.

3.

Across (continued)

7.

9.

10.

Down (continued)

4.

5.

8.

WORD CROSSES
Miscellaneous Grammar Topics

The word in the vertical column of each puzzle is related to the theme of the puzzle. If you have forgotten your Italian grammar, consult the Grammar Charts section at the back.

81. The Present Indicative of Irregular Verbs
(Il presente indicativo dei verbi irregolari)

As in the word crosses of the previous part, each clue consists of an Italian infinitive and a pronoun. The latter indicates the present indicative form you are required to figure out. If you know your irregular verbs, this puzzle will hardly pose a challenge.

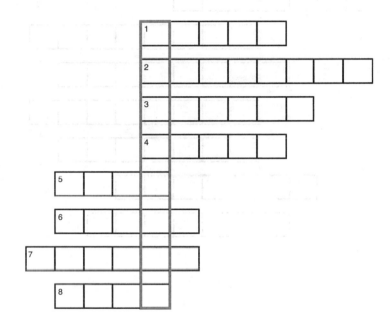

Clues

1. (potere) io ...

2. (riuscire) loro ...

3. (uscire) loro ...

4. (essere) voi ...

5. (dire) lei ...

6. (fare) loro ...

7. (sapere) voi ...

8. (dovere) lui ...

82. The Future and Conditional of Irregular Verbs
(Il futuro e il condizionale dei verbi irregolari)

As in the previous word cross puzzle, each clue consists of an Italian infinitive and a pronoun. The latter indicates the future or conditional form you are required to figure out.

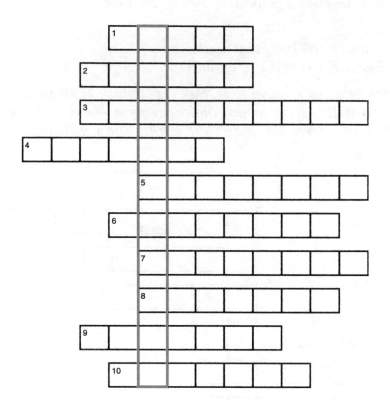

Clues

1. (dire) io ...

2. (fare) noi ...

3. (bere) loro ...

4. (sapere) voi ...

5. (guardare) io ...

6. (volere) noi ...

7. (lavare) voi ...

8. (avere) voi ...

9. (essere) loro ...

10. (dire) loro ...

83. Question Structures (Strutture interrogative)

The clues are interrogative sentences from which the required question words are missing.
This is certainly a challenging puzzle if you do not know how to ask questions!

Clues

1. ... è venuto ieri sera alla festa?

2. ... sei arrivato? Alle sette?

3. ... ti chiami?

4. ... non hai mangiato tutta la carne?

5. ... è quella donna?

6. ... sei andata ieri?

7. ... hai fatto in centro?

8. ... è costato il biglietto?

9. ... dolce preferisci?

84. Noun Plurals Again (Il plurale dei nomi ancora una volta)

As in puzzle 31, the clues are the singular forms of the required plural nouns. This is a challenging puzzle only if you do not know your noun plurals!

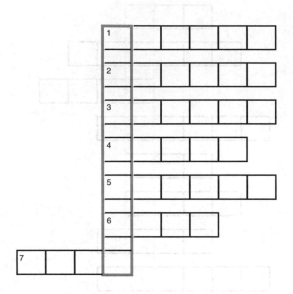

Clues

1. piazza

2. labbro

3. uomo

4. radio

5. amica

6. luce

7. mano

85. Adverbs (Gli avverbi)

The clues are sentences from which the required adverbs are missing.

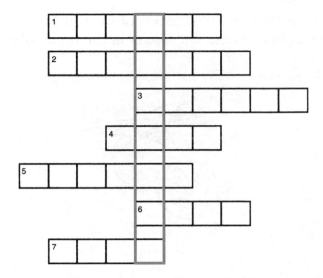

Clues

1. Loro arriveranno ...

2. Lui è ... molto bravo.

3. Loro abitano qui ...

4. Sono arrivati ...

5. Lei viene ... in ritardo.

6. Io sto molto ..., grazie.

7. Lo devi fare ..., non domani!

SCRAMBLED LETTERS
Travel and Transportation
(I viaggi e i trasporti)

The first column contains the scrambled letters of the word or expression to which the clue in the middle column applies. Write the answer in the third column by unscrambling the letters.

86. Cars (Le macchine)

Each clue either describes the automobile part or what it allows one to do.

Scrambled Letters	Clues	Answers
1. VLANOTE	permette di girare la macchina	_____
2. PMATINEUCO	si chiama anche "gomma"	_____
3. BULAE	dove si trova la ruota di scorta	_____
4. CANOOF	copre il motore	_____
5. PABREARZZA	vetro protettore	_____
6. PAURARTI	protegge la carrozzeria	_____
7. RFAI	le "luci" dell'auto	_____
8. FENRO	arresta il movimento della macchina	_____

87. Airports and Airplanes (Gli aeroporti e gli aerei)

Scrambled Letters	Clues	Answers
1. CRTAA D'IARCMBO	documento che permette al passeggero di imbarcarsi	_____
2. ATENTSSISE ID VOOL	la persona di servizio durante il volo	_____
3. COANTMANDE	il pilota	_____
4. LA FITRINNESO	posto dal quale si può vedere fuori	_____
5. CITURNA ID SIEZZCURA	si deve allacciare per il decollo e per l'atterraggio	_____
6. LA CODOIRRIO	posto vicino al "passaggio" dove si cammina in aereo	_____
7. DOLECLO	il contrario di atterraggio	_____

88. Trains and Buses (I treni e gli autobus)

Scrambled Letters	Clues	Answers
1. OARIOR	contiene indicazioni sugli arrivi e sulle partenze	_____
2. SIONETAZ FARIERROVIA	dove si deve andare per prendere il treno	_____
3. CLINEAPOA	dove si può prendere l'autobus	_____
4. FROVIERA	servizio di trasporto a mezzo di treni	_____
5. FREA LI BTTOIGLIE	cosa bisogna fare prima di poter viaggiare in treno	_____

89. Hotels (Gli alberghi)

Scrambled Letters	Clues	Answers
1. PANIO	ciascuno dei "livelli" in cui è diviso l'albergo	_____
2. PNOTAZREIONE	bisogna farla per essere sicuri di avere una camera	_____
3. CRTAA ID CDITREO	tessera usata per i pagamenti	_____
4. CAERMA	nome più comune per la stanza	_____
5. PINISCA	dove si va per nuotare	_____

90. Vacations (Le vacanze)

Scrambled Letters	Clues	Answers
1. ALL'EEROST	vacanza "in un paese straniero"	_____
2. LA AMRE	vacanza "in una zona dove si può nuotare"	_____
3. NI MTAGONNA	vacanza in una zona "elevata"	_____
4. AISMLPINO	attività che ha luogo "nelle montagne"	_____
5. PIONENSE	luogo che offre vitto e alloggio "a un prezzo stabilito"	_____

WORD SEARCHES
Computers and Technology (I computer e la tecnologia)

The hidden words can be read in one of three directions: from left to right, from right to left, and top down. Circle them.

91. Computers (I computer)

The clues are either synonyms or descriptions of computer components (screen, printer...).

A	B	T	C	D	E	F	G	H	I	L	M	P
S	T	A	M	P	A	N	T	E	E	F	G	O
C	M	S	C	D	E	F	G	H	I	L	M	R
H	L	T	C	A	D	S	D	M	L	D	L	T
E	T	I	R	M	O	U	S	E	R	S	T	A
R	M	E	C	D	E	F	G	H	I	L	M	T
M	L	R	C	A	D	S	D	M	L	D	L	I
O	M	A	C	D	E	F	G	H	I	L	M	L
S	L	T	C	A	D	S	D	M	L	D	L	E

Clues

1. produce copie
2. superficie sulla quale si riproducono le immagini
3. serie di tasti di un computer
4. dispositivo che permette di spostare il cursore
5. laptop

92. Television (La televisione)

The clues are descriptions of television concepts (program, remote control...).

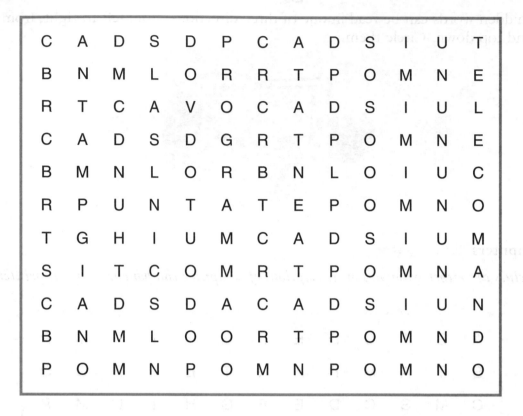

```
C   A   D   S   D   P   C   A   D   S   I   U   T
B   N   M   L   O   R   R   T   P   O   M   N   E
R   T   C   A   V   O   C   A   D   S   I   U   L
C   A   D   S   D   G   R   T   P   O   M   N   E
B   M   N   L   O   R   B   N   L   O   I   U   C
R   P   U   N   T   A   T   E   P   O   M   N   O
T   G   H   I   U   M   C   A   D   S   I   U   M
S   I   T   C   O   M   R   T   P   O   M   N   A
C   A   D   S   D   A   C   A   D   S   I   U   N
B   N   M   L   O   O   R   T   P   O   M   N   D
P   O   M   N   P   O   M   N   P   O   M   N   O
```

Clues

1. ciò che descrive il contenuto e il genere di una manifestazione televisiva
2. programma costituito da brevi commedie con gli stessi personaggi
3. programma "seriale" (programma a ...)
4. ricezione dei segnali televisivi via "corda"
5. dispositivo che permette di regolare il televisore

93. Internet (Internet)

The clues are either synonyms or descriptions of Internet concepts (e-mail, website...).

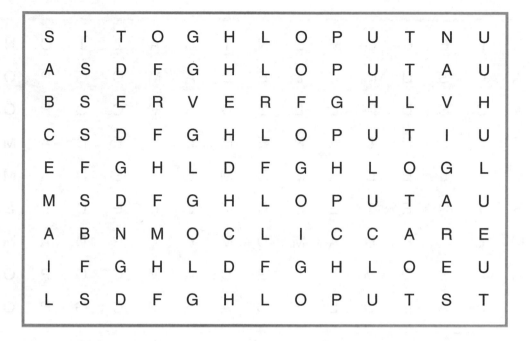

S	I	T	O	G	H	L	O	P	U	T	N	U
A	S	D	F	G	H	L	O	P	U	T	A	U
B	S	E	R	V	E	R	F	G	H	L	V	H
C	S	D	F	G	H	L	O	P	U	T	I	U
E	F	G	H	L	D	F	G	H	L	O	G	L
M	S	D	F	G	H	L	O	P	U	T	A	U
A	B	N	M	O	C	L	I	C	C	A	R	E
I	F	G	H	L	D	F	G	H	L	O	E	U
L	S	D	F	G	H	L	O	P	U	T	S	T

Clues

1. posta elettronica
2. "luogo" su Internet
3. il computer che raggruppa informazioni da altri computer per distribuirle su Internet
4. passare da sito a sito
5. premere il pulsante del mouse

94. Communications (Le telecomunicazioni)

The clues are either synonyms or descriptions of communication technology (cell phone, satellite dish...).

T	E	L	E	C	O	M	U	N	I	C	A	Z	I	O	N	I
C	A	D	S	D	M	L	L	E	D	A	M	C	G	P	O	B
C	A	D	S	D	M	L	L	E	D	A	M	C	G	P	O	B
C	E	L	L	U	L	A	R	E	M	L	L	E	D	A	M	D
A	M	L	L	E	D	A	M	D	M	L	L	E	D	A	M	D
V	R	T	R	E	T	E	S	D	M	L	L	E	D	L	E	D
O	M	L	L	E	D	A	M	D	M	L	L	R	D	A	M	D
C	A	D	S	D	M	L	L	E	D	A	M	C	G	P	O	B
P	A	R	A	B	O	L	I	C	A	A	M	C	G	P	O	B

Clues

1. telefono portatile
2. antenna che permette di ricevere trasmissioni a grande distanza (antenna ...)
3. trasmissione per via di "corde grosse" (trasmissione via ...)
4. insieme di computer collegati tra loro
5. comunicazioni a distanza

95. The Phone (Il telefono)

The clues are either synonyms or descriptions of phone concepts (subscriber, long-distance...).

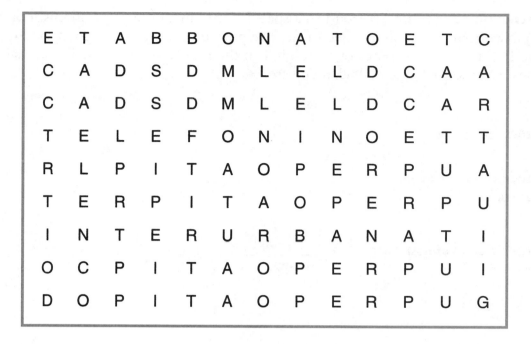

```
E  T  A  B  B  O  N  A  T  O  E  T  C
C  A  D  S  D  M  L  E  L  D  C  A  A
C  A  D  S  D  M  L  E  L  D  C  A  R
T  E  L  E  F  O  N  I  N  O  E  T  T
R  L  P  I  T  A  O  P  E  R  P  U  A
T  E  R  P  I  T  A  O  P  E  R  P  U
I  N  T  E  R  U  R  B  A  N  A  T  I
O  C  P  I  T  A  O  P  E  R  P  U  I
D  O  P  I  T  A  O  P  E  R  P  U  G
```

Clues

1. chi ha fatto un abbonamento
2. comunicazione telefonica tra posti lontani
3. sinonimo popolare per "cellulare"
4. pubblicazione che contiene i numeri di telefono degli abbonati (... telefonico)
5. tessera prepagata (... telefonica)

CRYPTOGRAMS
Italian Culture (Cultura italiana)

A specific number will correspond to a specific letter in all the cryptograms. For example, if you establish that 1 = H in any one of the five puzzles, then you can go ahead and substitute H for each occurrence of the digit 1 in the remaining puzzles. These challenging puzzles test your knowledge of Italian culture.

96. Writers (Scrittori)

1. l'autore della *Divina Commedia*

$\overline{1} \quad \overline{2} \quad \overline{3} \quad \overline{4} \quad \overline{5}$

2. l'autore dei *Promessi Sposi* (Alessandro ...)

$\overline{6} \quad \overline{2} \quad \overline{3} \quad \overline{7} \quad \overline{8} \quad \overline{3} \quad \overline{9}$

97. Artists (Artisti)

1. l'artista che ho scolpito il David

$\overline{6} \quad \overline{9} \quad \overline{10} \quad \overline{11} \quad \overline{5} \quad \overline{12} \quad \overline{2} \quad \overline{3} \quad \overline{13} \quad \overline{5} \quad \overline{12} \quad \overline{8}$

2. grande artista e scienziato (Leonardo ...)

$\overline{1} \quad \overline{2} \qquad \overline{14} \quad \overline{9} \quad \overline{3} \quad \overline{10} \quad \overline{9}$

98. Musicians (Musicisti)

1. il compositore della *Traviata* (Giuseppe ...)

$\overline{14} \quad \overline{5} \quad \overline{15} \quad \overline{1} \quad \overline{9}$

2. il compositore del *Barbiere di Siviglia* (Gioacchino ...)

$\overline{15} \quad \overline{8} \quad \overline{16} \quad \overline{16} \quad \overline{9} \quad \overline{3} \quad \overline{9}$

99. Film Directors (Registi)

1. il regista del film *8½*
   (Federico ...)

   $\overline{17}$ $\overline{5}$ $\overline{12}$ $\overline{12}$ $\overline{9}$ $\overline{3}$ $\overline{9}$

2. il regista del film *Nuovo
   cinema paradiso* (Giuseppe ...)

   $\overline{4}$ $\overline{8}$ $\overline{15}$ $\overline{3}$ $\overline{2}$ $\overline{4}$ $\overline{8}$ $\overline{15}$ $\overline{5}$

100. Famous Cities (Città famose)

1. la città eterna

   $\overline{15}$ $\overline{8}$ $\overline{6}$ $\overline{2}$

2. la città dove nacque il
   Rinascimento

   $\overline{17}$ $\overline{9}$ $\overline{15}$ $\overline{5}$ $\overline{3}$ $\overline{7}$ $\overline{5}$

Answers

1.

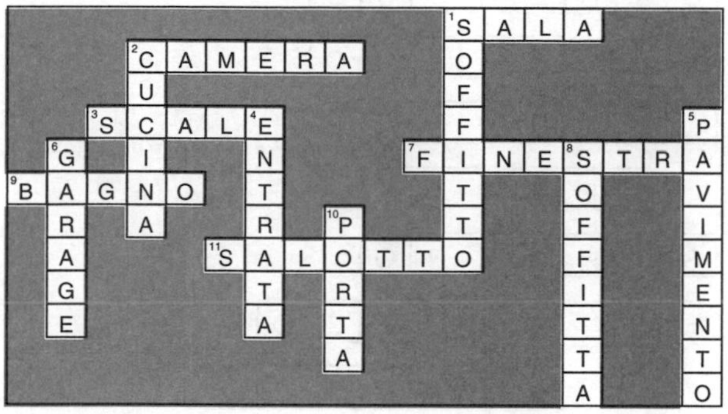

Across/Down answers: SALA · CAMERA · CUCINA · SCALE · ENTRATA · GARAGE · BAGNO · FINESTRA · SOFFITTA · PORTA · SALOTTO · PAVIMENTO · P

2.

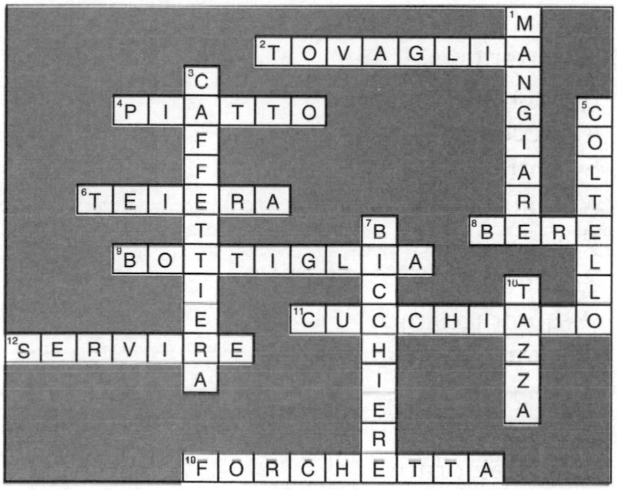

MANGIARE · TOVAGLIA · CAFFETTIERA · PIATTO · COLTELLO · TEIERA · BERE · BOTTIGLIA · BICCHIERE · CUCCHIAIO · TAZZA · SERVIRE · FORCHETTA

3.

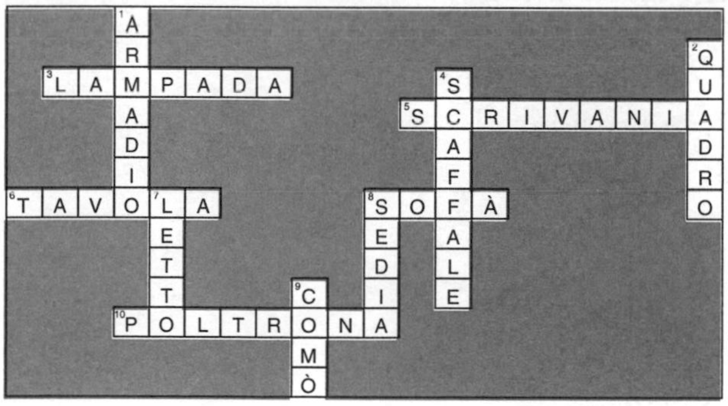

ARMADIO · QUADRO · LAMPADA · SCAFFALE · SCRIVANIA · TAVOLA · LETTO · SOFÀ · SEDIA · COMÒ · POLTRONA

4.

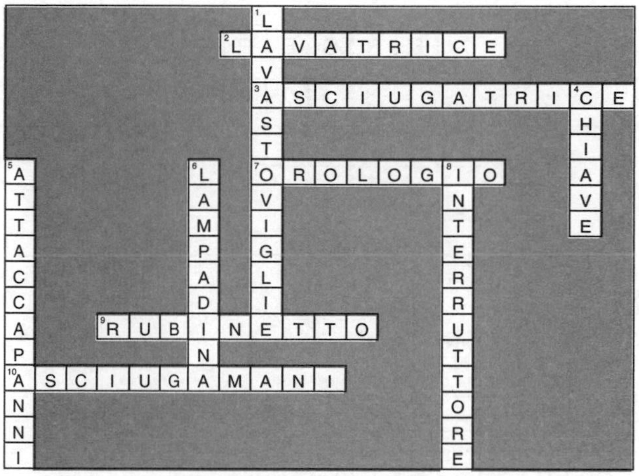

LAVASTOVIGLIE · LAVATRICE · ASCIUGATRICE · CHIAVE · ATTACCAPANNI · LAMPADINA · OROLOGIO · INTERRUTTORE · RUBINETTO · ASCIUGAMANI

5.

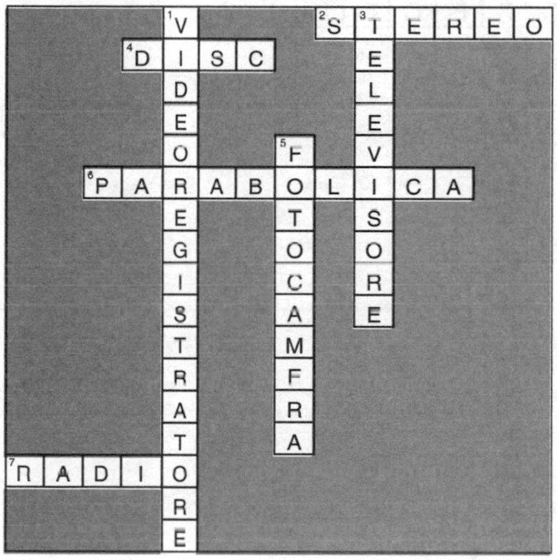

VIDEOREGISTRATORE · STEREO · DISC · TELEVISORE · FOTOCAMERA · PARABOLICA · RADIO

6.

MADRE · ZIA · FRATELLO · SORELLA · PADRE · NONNI · ZIO · CUGINETTI · PAPÀ

95

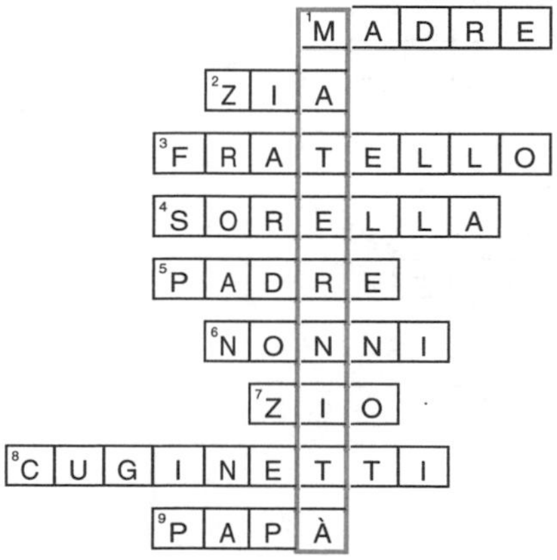

7.

```
          ¹P O P O L O
²R A G A Z Z E
          ³R A G A Z Z I
        ⁴E S S E R E
          ⁵U O M O
          ⁶D O N N A
        ⁷G E N T E
```

8.

```
  ¹M A N O
    ²N A S O
  ³B R A C C I O
    ⁴T E S T A
    ⁵O R E C C H I O
  ⁶G A M B A
    ⁷P I E D E
  ⁸O C C H I O
    ⁹B O C C A
```

9.

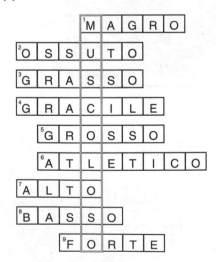

```
    ¹M A G R O
  ²O S S U T O
  ³G R A S S O
  ⁴G R A C I L E
    ⁵G R O S S O
    ⁶A T L E T I C O
  ⁷A L T O
  ⁸B A S S O
    ⁹F O R T E
```

10.

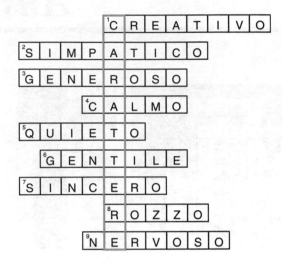

```
        ¹C R E A T I V O
²S I M P A T I C O
³G E N E R O S O
        ⁴C A L M O
⁵Q U I E T O
        ⁶G E N T I L E
⁷S I N C E R O
          ⁸R O Z Z O
        ⁹N E R V O S O
```

11.
1. dodici
2. settanta
3. ottanta
4. trecento
5. un terzo
6. mille
7. un milione
8. primo
9. quindicesimo
10. ventunesimo

12.
1. mezzogiorno
2. mezzanotte
3. l'una e cinque
4. l'una e mezzo
5. le due e un quarto
6. le dieci del mattino
7. le ventidue
8. le quattordici

13.
1. nuvoloso
2. coperto
3. sole
4. vento
5. freddo
6. caldo
7. piove
8. nevica

14.
1. rosso
2. azzurro
3. verde
4. giallo
5. marrone
6. viola
7. rosa
8. bianco
9. nero
10. arancione

15.
1. dolce
2. amaro
3. duro
4. molle
5. rotondo
6. liscio
7. ondulato
8. bagnato
9. asciutto

16.

Q	A	P	E	R	T	U	I	O	P	L	G	A
S	C	A	P	P	E	L	L	O	D	T	I	I
Z	C	N	C	N	T	U	I	O	P	L	A	3
Q	P	T	S	C	D	F	G	H	L	O	C	O
C	R	A	V	A	T	T	A	R	T	U	C	O
T	T	L	I	M	T	U	I	O	P	L	A	L
O	O	O	O	I	O	V	O	M	C	A	D	3
P	P	N	P	C	P	E	P	A	C	A	D	S
M	M	I	M	I	M	S	M	G	O	N	N	A
N	N	P	N	A	N	T	N	L	C	A	D	S
B	B	M	B	S	B	I	B	I	C	A	D	S
C	A	M	I	C	E	T	T	A	C	A	D	S
A	S	D	G	C	O	O	I	L	O	P	T	V

1. pantaloni
2. cappello
3. cravatta
4. giacca
5. camicia
6. camicetta

7. gonna
8. vestito
9. maglia

17.

Q	E	R	T	A	S	U	O	L	A	C	U	S
Q	E	R	T	A	T	G	H	U	I	O	P	A
A	C	A	L	Z	I	N	O	L	O	D	C	N
S	A	L	O	D	V	G	H	U	I	O	P	D
D	L	U	I	O	A	G	H	U	I	O	P	A
F	Z	U	I	O	L	G	H	U	I	O	P	L
G	A	U	I	O	E	B	N	T	A	C	C	O
H	A	S	D	R	E	T	U	I	O	P	L	I
L	A	S	A	P	R	A	C	S	D	C	U	I

1. stivale
2. calzino
3. scarpa
4. calza
5. sandalo
6. tacco
7. suola

18.

A	N	E	L	L	O	A	R	D	G	N	M	O
V	C	U	I	O	R	B	N	M	C	C	H	U
C	D	A	S	C	O	L	L	A	N	A	T	R
P	S	R	T	I	C	D	A	S	T	H	U	U
V	C	U	I	O	O	C	D	A	S	E	M	O
P	S	R	T	I	G	C	D	A	S	N	T	R
R	D	G	S	P	I	L	L	A	Q	A	H	U
V	C	U	I	O	O	V	C	U	I	O	T	R
P	S	R	T	I	V	C	U	I	O	P	M	O
O	R	E	C	C	H	I	N	O	T	R	H	U

1. orologio
2. anello
3. collana
4. catena
5. orecchino
6. spilla

19.

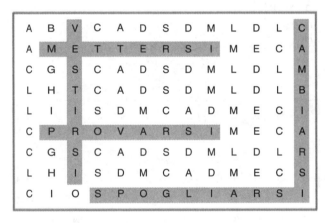

1. borsa
2. guanto
3. sciarpa
4. cintura
5. bottone
6. portafoglio

20.

A	B	V	C	A	D	S	D	M	L	D	L	C
A	M	E	T	T	E	R	S	I	M	E	C	A
C	G	S	C	A	D	S	D	M	L	D	L	M
L	H	T	C	A	D	S	D	M	L	D	L	B
L	I	I	S	D	M	C	A	D	M	E	C	I
C	P	R	O	V	A	R	S	I	M	E	C	A
C	G	S	C	A	D	S	D	M	L	D	L	R
L	H	I	S	D	M	C	A	D	M	E	C	S
C	I	O	S	P	O	G	L	I	A	R	S	I

1. vestirsi
2. mettersi
3. cambiarsi
4. spogliarsi
5. provarsi

21.

1. Ciao!
2. Arrivederci!

22.

1. Mi chiamo …
2. Piacere!

23.

1. nome
2. cognome

24.

1. strada
2. Abito in via …

25.

1. Pronto!
2. (numero) telefonico

26.

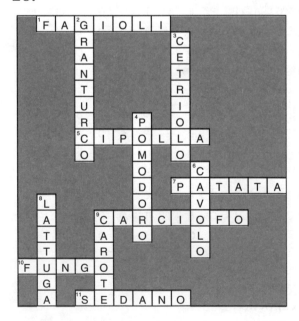

27.

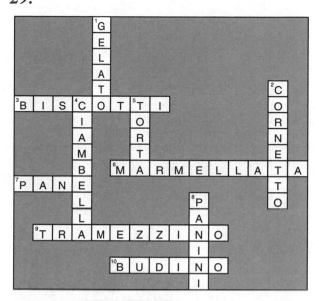

29.

28.

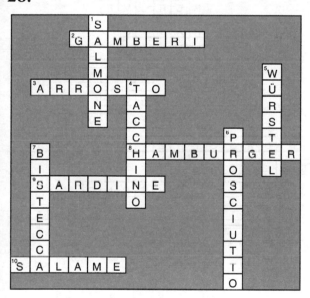

30.

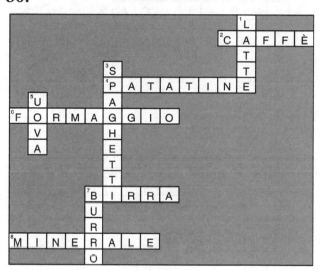

31.

	P	I	A	N	I
	L	U	O	G	H	I
	C	U	O	C	H	I
G	I	O	R	N	A	L	I
	A	M	I	C	I
F	A	L	C	H	I
G	R	E	C	I

32.

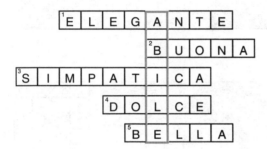

E	L	E	G	A	N	T	E
	B	U	O	N	A
S	I	M	P	A	T	I	C	A
	D	O	L	C	E
	B	E	L	L	A

33.

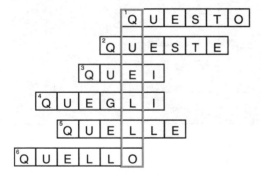

Q	U	E	S	T	O
Q	U	E	S	T	E
Q	U	E	I
Q	U	E	G	L	I
Q	U	E	L	L	E
Q	U	E	L	L	O

34.

P	A	C	C	O
N	O	S	T	R	E
S	U	O
S	U	A
M	I	E
S	U	O	I
S	U	E
T	U	O	I
V	O	S	T	R	I
L	O	R	O

35.

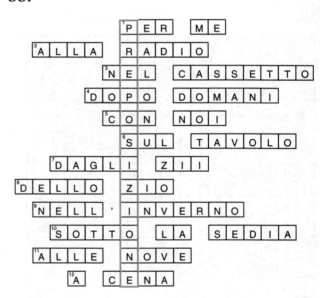

P	E	R		M	E
A	L	L	A		R	A	D	I	O
N	E	L		C	A	S	S	E	T	T	O
D	O	P	O		D	O	M	A	N	I
C	O	N		N	O	I
S	U	L		T	A	V	O	L	O
D	A	G	L	I		Z	I	I
D	E	L	L	O		Z	I	O
N	E	L	L	'	I	N	V	E	R	N	O
S	O	T	T	O		L	A		S	E	D	I	A
A	L	L	E		N	O	V	E
A		C	E	N	A

36.
1. bere
2. acqua
3. sete
4. Alla salute!
5. vino
6. bevanda analcolica
7. limonata
8. aranciata

37.
1. menu
2. mancia
3. cameriere
4. cameriera
5. piatto
6. porzione
7. prenotazione

38.
1. mangiare
2. tagliare
3. assaggiare
4. versare
5. servire
6. prendere
7. digerire
8. vomitare

39.
1. salato
2. piccante
3. dolce
4. alla griglia
5. arrostito
6. al forno
7. maturo
8. aspro

40.
1. ben cotto
2. al sugo
3. insalata di riso
4. antipasto
5. frutti di mare
6. patate fritte

41.

D	O	P	E	A	D	C	D	S	L	P	T	C
P	E	N	D	O	L	A	R	E	A	E	I	E
E	F	G	I	R	T	U	I	P	O	R	O	N
D	O	P	F	A	D	C	D	S	L	I	P	T
E	F	G	I	R	T	U	I	P	O	F	E	R
D	O	P	C	A	P	I	T	A	L	E	R	O
E	F	G	I	A	D	C	D	S	L	R	S	P
E	T	N	O	P	D	C	D	S	L	I	D	E
A	D	C	D	S	L	U	I	P	O	A	V	R

1. edificio
2. ponte
3. capitale
4. periferia
5. pendolare
6. centro

42.

A	S	S	B	N	M	L	O	P	P	L	O	P
P	R	E	C	E	D	E	N	Z	A	B	N	M
C	D	M	B	N	M	L	O	P	R	L	O	P
A	S	A	C	D	P	B	N	M	C	A	S	D
C	D	F	A	S	U	L	O	P	H	L	O	P
A	S	O	A	S	N	A	S	D	I	B	N	M
F	E	R	M	A	T	A	B	L	M	L	O	P
A	S	O	C	D	A	S	D	F	E	A	S	D
B	N	M	L	O	P	M	L	O	T	M	L	O
T	S	O	R	P	A	S	S	A	R	E	B	L
B	N	M	L	O	P	M	L	O	O	A	S	D

1. semaforo
2. precedenza
3. parchimetro
4. fermata
5. sorpassare
6. punta

43.

M	A	R	C	I	A	P	I	E	D	E	C	V	B	V
S	D	A	D	C	U	O	S	D	C	V	B	A	S	I
S	D	A	D	C	T	G	H	I	O	L	P	P	O	C
L	S	O	T	T	O	P	A	S	S	A	G	G	I	O
G	T	S	D	G	S	O	S	D	C	V	B	A	S	L
H	R	O	S	D	T	N	I	N	C	R	O	C	I	O
N	A	S	D	G	R	G	H	I	O	L	P	P	O	N
M	D	O	S	D	A	O	S	D	C	V	B	A	S	M
L	A	S	D	G	D	G	H	I	O	L	P	P	O	L
O	S	D	G	H	A	O	S	D	C	V	B	A	S	O

1. strada
2. vicolo
3. incrocio
4. marciapiede
5. sottopassaggio
6. autostrada

44.

T	A	S	D	C	D	S	M	C	A	D	S	D	
R	F	R	E	C	C	A	U	D	F	G	O	M	
I	S	I	E	H	B	N	S	C	A	D	S	D	
B	I	B	L	I	O	T	E	C	A	A	G	H	
U	S	I	E	E	D	S	O	C	A	D	S	D	
N	F	R	E	S	C	A	E	D	F	G	O	M	
A	S	I	E	A	S	I	E	C	A	D	S	D	
L	F	R	E	C	A	D	S	D	A	E	I	O	
E	D	G	N	E	G	O	Z	I	O	U	P	O	

1. chiesa
2. museo
3. biblioteca
4. tribunale
5. negozio

45.

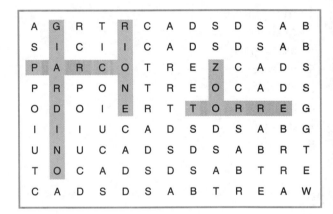

A	G	R	T	R	C	A	D	S	D	S	A	B
S	I	C	I	I	C	A	D	S	D	S	A	B
P	A	R	C	O	T	R	E	Z	C	A	D	S
P	R	P	O	N	T	R	E	O	C	A	D	S
O	D	O	I	E	R	T	T	O	R	R	E	G
I	I	I	U	C	A	D	S	D	S	A	B	G
U	N	U	C	A	D	S	D	S	A	B	R	T
T	O	C	A	D	S	D	S	A	B	T	R	E
C	A	D	S	D	S	A	B	T	R	E	A	W

1. parco
2. giardino
3. rione
4. torre
5. zoo

46.
1. Grazie!
2. Prego!

47.
1. Scusi!
2. Per favore!

48.
1. Basta!
2. Non ci credo!

49.
1. Certo!
2. Impossibile!

50.
1. Va bene!
2. Magari!

51.

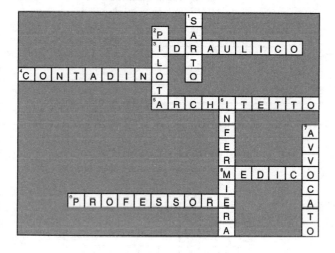

52.

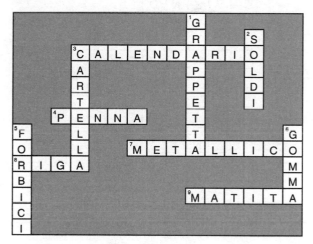

53.

54.

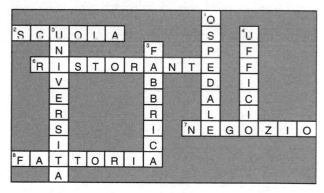

55.

58.

56.

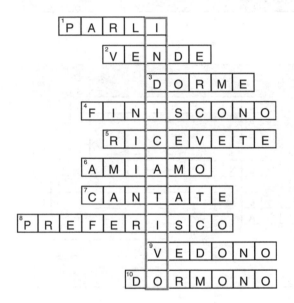

59.

57.

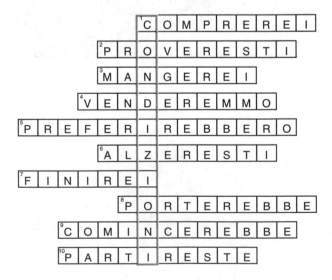

60.

61.

1. baseball
2. football americano
3. pallacanestro
4. tennis
5. hockey
6. calcio
7. golf
8. ginnastica
9. sci

62.

1. ghiaccio
2. stadio
3. campo
4. palestra
5. pista

63.

1. dama
2. scacchi
3. carte da gioco
4. parole crociate
5. puzzle

64.

1. fare delle spese
2. andare al cinema
3. passatempo
4. lettura
5. fare una passeggiata
6. nuotare

65.

1. campeggio
2. vacanze
3. esercitarsi
4. praticare gli sport
5. fare il jogging

66.

S	A	D	G	H	L	O	I	M	N	O	P	G	A	A
O	P	E	R	A	Z	I	O	N	E	M	N	O	M
C	M	N	O	G	H	L	A	D	G	M	N	O	B
C	A	D	G	H	L	O	I	M	N	O	P	G	U
O	M	N	O	G	H	L	A	D	G	M	N	O	L
R	I	A	N	I	M	A	Z	I	O	N	E	U	A
S	A	D	G	H	L	O	I	M	N	O	P	G	N
O	B	M	A	T	E	R	N	I	T	À	G	I	Z
P	A	D	G	H	L	O	I	M	N	O	P	G	A

1. rianimazione
2. operazione
3. maternità
4. ambulanza
5. soccorso

67.

C	A	D	S	E	F	B	R	T	U	I	O	I
C	A	D	S	E	E	U	I	O	D	L	P	N
B	R	T	U	I	B	B	R	T	O	R	T	F
B	R	T	U	I	B	B	R	T	L	O	P	L
A	M	B	N	M	R	U	I	O	O	D	G	U
R	A	F	F	R	E	D	D	O	R	E	O	E
U	L	B	R	T	U	I	O	I	E	D	P	N
C	A	D	S	R	T	U	I	O	T	D	G	Z
R	T	T	T	C	C	B	B	R	R	R	T	A

1. febbre
2. dolore
3. mal
4. raffreddore
5. influenza

68.

R	T	C	C	D	S	A	S	D	L	D	M	D
E	C	A	V	I	T	À	E	A	U	E	U	A
A	A	R	S	D	L	R	T	U	I	N	I	U
U	U	I	C	D	S	A	S	D	L	T	L	D
B	B	E	S	D	L	R	T	U	I	I	I	O
G	G	D	C	D	S	A	S	D	L	E	L	D
I	M	P	I	O	M	B	A	T	U	R	A	P
G	G	D	C	D	S	A	S	D	L	A	D	F
I	N	I	E	Z	I	O	N	E	A	S	D	L

1. cavità
2. impiombatura
3. carie
4. iniezione
5. dentiera

70.

A	U	S	I	L	I	A	R	E	A	D	R	P
C	A	D	S	D	S	M	L	L	E	D	A	O
A	G	G	R	E	S	S	O	R	E	E	R	M
C	A	D	S	D	S	M	L	L	E	D	A	P
A	L	C	A	D	S	D	S	M	L	L	E	I
D	A	D	S	D	S	M	L	L	E	D	A	E
T	D	D	S	D	S	M	L	L	E	D	A	R
E	R	D	S	D	S	M	L	L	E	D	A	E
P	O	L	I	Z	I	O	T	T	O	D	T	H

1. ladro
2. poliziotto
3. pompiere
4. ausiliare
5. aggressore

69.

S	T	A	R	N	U	T	I	R	E	H	H	A
S	D	A	C	S	D	M	L	E	P	O	B	L
S	D	A	C	S	D	M	L	E	P	O	B	L
G	I	R	A	M	E	N	T	O	C	S	D	E
S	D	A	C	S	D	A	S	D	A	C	S	R
C	S	D	M	L	E	U	M	L	E	P	O	G
S	D	A	C	S	D	S	M	L	E	P	O	I
T	O	S	S	I	R	E	S	D	A	C	S	A
Q	R	T	U	I	O	A	B	H	I	T	G	M

1. tossire
2. giramento
3. nausea
4. allergia
5. starnutire

71.
1. tagliare
2. parrucchiere

72.
1. smalto
2. trucco

73.
1. gioia
2. tristezza

74.
1. fantasia
2. stupidità

75.
1. egoista
2. altruista

76.

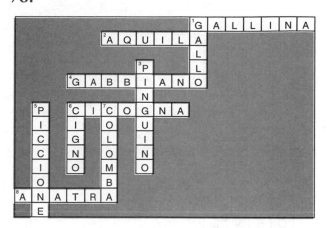

FIORI · ERBACCIA · FOGLIA · RAMO · STELO · SEMENZA · ALBERO · RADICE

78.

GALLINA · GALLO · AQUILA · PINGUINO · GABBIANO · PICCIONE · CIGNO · CICOGNA · COLOMBA · ANATRA · E

77.

GIRAFFA · GORILLA · ASINO · MUCCA · BUFALO · TOPO · SCIMMIA · MONTONE · PECORA · CAVALLO · ORSO · LEONE · CAPRA · CERVO · ELEFANTE · CASTORO

79.

QUERCIA · ULIVO · CASTAGNO · ACERO · CILIEGIO · MELO · ABETE · PERO

80.

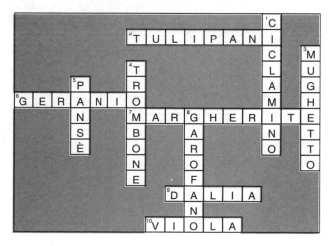

CICLAMINO · TULIPANI · MUGHETTO · TROMBONE · PANSÈ · GERANIO · MARGHERITE · GAROFANO · DALIA · VIOLA

81.

82.

83.

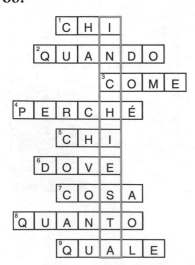

84.

85.

86.

1. volante
2. pneumatico
3. baule
4. cofano
5. parabrezza
6. paraurti
7. fari
8. freno

87.

1. carta d'imbarco
2. assistente di volo
3. comandante
4. al finestrino
5. cintura di sicurezza
6. al corridoio
7. decollo

88.
1. orario
2. stazione ferroviaria
3. capolinea
4. ferrovia
5. fare il biglietto

89.
1. piano
2. prenotazione
3. carta di credito
4. camera
5. piscina

90.
1. all'estero
2. al mare
3. in montagna
4. alpinismo
5. pensione

91.

A	B	T	C	D	E	F	G	H	I	L	M	P
S	T	A	M	P	A	N	T	E	E	F	G	O
C	M	S	C	D	E	F	G	H	I	L	M	R
H	L	T	C	A	D	S	D	M	L	D	L	T
E	T	I	R	M	O	U	S	E	R	S	T	A
R	M	E	C	D	E	F	G	H	I	L	M	T
M	L	R	C	A	D	S	D	M	L	D	L	I
O	M	A	C	D	E	F	G	H	I	I	M	I
S	L	T	C	A	D	S	D	M	L	D	L	E

1. stampante
2. schermo
3. tastiera
4. mouse
5. portatile

92.

C	A	D	S	D	P	C	A	D	S	I	U	T
B	N	M	L	O	R	R	T	P	O	M	N	E
R	T	C	A	V	O	C	A	D	S	I	U	L
C	A	D	S	D	G	R	T	P	O	M	N	E
B	M	N	L	O	R	B	N	L	O	I	U	C
R	P	U	N	T	A	T	E	P	O	M	N	O
T	G	H	I	U	M	C	A	D	S	I	U	M
S	I	T	C	O	M	R	T	P	O	M	N	A
C	A	D	S	D	A	C	A	D	S	I	U	N
B	N	M	L	O	O	R	T	P	O	M	N	D
P	O	M	N	P	O	M	N	P	O	M	N	O

1. programma
2. sitcom
3. puntate
4. cavo
5. telecomando

93.

S	I	T	O	G	H	L	O	P	U	T	N	U
A	S	D	F	G	H	L	O	P	U	T	A	U
B	S	E	R	V	E	R	F	G	H	L	V	H
C	S	D	F	G	H	L	O	P	U	T	I	U
E	F	G	H	L	D	F	G	H	L	O	G	L
M	S	D	F	G	H	L	O	P	U	T	A	U
A	B	N	M	O	C	L	I	C	C	A	R	E
I	F	G	H	L	D	F	G	H	L	O	E	U
L	S	D	F	G	H	L	O	P	U	T	S	T

1. email
2. sito
3. server
4. navigare
5. cliccare

94.

T	E	L	E	C	O	M	U	N	I	C	A	Z	I	O	N	I	I
C	A	D	S	D	M	L	L	E	D	A	M	C	G	P	O	B	
C	A	D	S	D	M	L	L	E	D	A	M	C	G	P	O	B	
C	E	L	L	U	L	A	R	E	M	L	L	E	D	A	M	D	
A	M	L	L	E	D	A	M	D	M	L	L	E	D	A	M	D	
V	R	T	R	E	T	E	S	D	M	L	L	E	D	L	E	D	
O	M	L	L	E	D	A	M	D	M	L	L	R	D	A	M	D	
C	A	D	S	D	M	L	L	E	D	A	M	C	G	P	O	B	
P	A	R	A	B	O	L	I	C	A	A	M	C	G	P	O	B	

1. cellulare
2. parabolica
3. cavo
4. rete
5. telecomunicazioni

95.

E	T	A	B	B	O	N	A	T	O	E	T	C
C	A	D	S	D	M	L	E	L	D	C	A	A
C	A	D	S	D	M	L	E	L	D	C	A	R
T	E	L	E	F	O	N	I	N	O	E	T	T
R	L	P	I	T	A	O	P	E	R	P	U	A
T	E	R	P	I	T	A	O	P	E	R	P	U
I	N	T	E	R	U	R	B	A	N	A	T	I
O	C	P	I	T	A	O	P	E	R	P	U	I
D	O	P	I	T	A	O	P	E	R	P	U	G

1. abbonato
2. interurbana
3. telefonino
4. elenco
5. carta

96.
1. Dante
2. Manzoni

97.
1. Michelangelo
2. Da Vinci

98.
1. Verdi
2. Rossini

99.
1. Fellini
2. Tornatore

100.
1. Roma
2. Firenze

Grammar Charts

Certain puzzles entail knowing the contents of the following charts, which do not contain complete information about Italian grammar. They have been designed simply to help you solve the puzzles.

Noun Plurals (Puzzles 31 and 84)

1. The plural of regular masculine nouns is formed by changing the last vowel (be it o or e) to i. If the noun ends in co it changes to ci, if e or i precede, otherwise it changes to chi; and if it ends in go it generally changes to ghi, except in some special cases. The rule regarding co and go is really only a guideline. There are a number of exceptions to it.

Singular		Plural	
(il) piano	floor	(i) piani	floors
(il) giornale	newspaper	(i) giornali	newspapers
(il) luogo	place	(i) luoghi	places
(l') amico	friend	(gli) amici	friends
(il) cuoco	cook	(i) cuochi	cooks
(il) falco	falcon	(i) falchi	falcons
(il) greco	Greek	(i) greci	Greeks

2. The plural of regular feminine nouns is formed by changing the final a to e or the final e to i. If the noun ends in ca or ga it changes to che and ghe respectively.

Singular		Plural	
(la) piazza	town square	(le) piazze	town squares
(la) luce	light	(le) luci	lights
(l') amica	girlfriend	(le) amiche	girlfriends
(la) collega	colleague	(le) colleghe	colleagues

3. Note the plural of the following nouns:

Singular		Plural	
(l') uomo	man	(gli) uomini	men
(la) mano	hand	(le) mani	hands
(il) labbro	lip	(le) labbra	lips
(la) radio	radio	(le) radio	radios

Adjectives (Puzzle 32)

In Italian, adjectives are given in their masculine form in dictionaries. Generally speaking, if the masculine adjective ends in e, so too does the corresponding feminine adjective; if it ends in o, however, the corresponding feminine form is changed to a:

Masculine		Feminine	
elegante	elegant	elegante	elegant
dolce	sweet	dolce	sweet
bello	beautiful	bella	beautiful
simpatico	nice	simpatica	nice
buono	good	buona	good

Demonstrative Adjectives (Puzzle 33)

1. The English demonstratives *this/these* are rendered by questo, which changes its ending according to the gender and number:

Masculine Singular		Masculine Plural	
questo libro	this book	questi libri	these books
questo cane	this dog	questi cani	these dogs

Feminine Singular		Feminine Plural	
questa porta	this door	queste porte	these doors
questa finestra	this window	queste finestre	these windows

2. The English demonstrative *that/those* is rendered by quello, which changes its forms as shown:

Masculine Singular		Masculine Plural	
Before z or s + *consonant*			
quello zio	that uncle	quegli zii	those uncles
quello studente	that student	quegli studenti	those students
Before any other consonant			
quel libro	that book	quei libri	those books
quel gatto	that cat	quei gatti	those cats
Before any vowel			
quell'amico	that friend	quegli amici	those friends
quell'orologio	that watch	quegli orologi	those watches

Feminine Singular		Feminine Plural	
Before any consonant			
quella porta	that door	quelle porte	those doors
Before any vowel			
quell'amica	that friend	quelle amiche	those friends

Possessive Adjectives (Puzzle 34)

(fam. = familiar form, pol. = polite form, pl. = plural form)

Masculine Singular		Masculine Plural	
il mio libro	my book	i miei libri	my books
il tuo gatto (fam.)	your cat	i tuoi gatti	your cats
il suo cappotto	his/her coat	i suoi cappotti	his/her coats
il suo gatto (pol.)	your cat	i suoi gatti	your cats
il nostro libro	our book	i nostri libri	our books
il vostro amico (pol.)	your friend	i vostri amici	your friends
il loro corso	their course	i loro corsi	their courses

Feminine Singular		Feminine Plural	
la mia penna	my pen	le mie penne	my pens
la tua amica (fam.)	your friend	le tue amiche	your friends
la sua giacca	his/her jacket	le sue giacche	his/her jackets
la sua amica (pol.)	your friend	le sue amiche	your friends
la nostra penna	our pen	le nostre penne	our pens
la vostra amica (pol.)	your friend	le vostre amiche	your friends
la loro classe	their class	le loro classi	their classes

Prepositions (Puzzle 35)

Italian	English
a	at, to
dopo	after
con	with
da	from
in	in
di	of
per	for
sotto	under
su	on

Note the following prepositional contractions:

+	il	i	lo	l'	gli	la	le
a	al	ai	allo	all'	agli	alla	alle
in	nel	nei	nello	nell'	negli	nella	nelle
di	del	dei	dello	dell'	degli	della	delle
da	dal	dai	dallo	dall'	dagli	dalla	dalle
su	sul	sui	sullo	sull'	sugli	sulla	sulle

Question Structures (Puzzle 83)

Italian	English
chi	who
che/cosa	what
dove	where
perché	why
come	how
quanto	how much
quando	when
quale	which

Sample Conjugations of Regular Verbs (Puzzles 56, 57, 58, 59, 60)

1st Conjugation: amare / to love

Singular	Plural	Singular	Plural
Present Indicative		*Present Perfect*	
io amo (I love)	noi amiamo (we love)	io ho amato (I loved)	noi abbiamo amato (we loved)
tu ami (you love)	voi amate (you love)	tu hai amato (you loved)	voi avete amato (you loved)
lui/lei ama (he/she loves)	loro amano (they love)	lui/lei ha amato (he/she loved)	loro hanno amato (they loved)
Imperfect Indicative		*Future*	
io amavo (I was loving)	noi amavamo (we were loving)	io amerò (I will love)	noi ameremo (we will love)
tu amavi (you were loving)	voi amavate (you were loving)	tu amerai (you will love)	voi amerete (you will love)
lui/lei amava (he/she was loving)	loro amavano (they were loving)	lui/lei amerà (he/she will love)	loro ameranno (they will love)
Conditional			
io amerei (I would love)	noi ameremmo (we would love)		
tu ameresti (you would love)	voi amereste (you would love)		
lui/lei amerebbe (he/she would love)	loro amerebbero (they would love)		

2nd Conjugation: ricevere / to receive

Singular	Plural	Singular	Plural
Present Indicative		**Present Perfect**	
io ricevo (I receive)	noi riceviamo (we receive)	io ho ricevuto (I received)	noi abbiamo ricevuto (we received)
tu ricevi (you receive)	voi ricevete (you receive)	tu hai ricevuto (you received)	voi avete ricevuto (you received)
lui/lei riceve (he/she receives)	loro ricevono (they receive)	lui/lei ha ricevuto (he/she received)	loro hanno ricevuto (they received)
Imperfect Indicative		**Future**	
io ricevevo (I was receiving)	noi ricevevamo (we were receiving)	io riceverò (I will receive)	noi riceveremo (we will receive)
tu ricevevi (you were receiving)	voi ricevevate (you were receiving)	tu riceverai (you will receive)	voi riceverete (you will receive)
lui/lei riceveva (he/she was receiving)	loro ricevevano (they were receiving)	lui/lei riceverà (he/she will receive)	loro riceveranno (they will receive)
Conditional			
io riceverei (I would receive)	noi riceveremmo (we would receive)		
tu riceveresti (you would receive)	voi ricevereste (you would receive)		
lui/lei riceverebbe (he/she would receive)	loro riceverebbero (they would receive)		

3rd Conjugation: dormire / to sleep

Singular	Plural	Singular	Plural
Present Indicative		*Present Perfect*	
io dormo (I sleep)	noi dormiamo (we sleep)	io ho dormito (I slept)	noi abbiamo dormito (we slept)
tu dormi (you sleep)	voi dormite (you sleep)	tu hai dormito (you slept)	voi avete dormito (you slept)
lui/lei dorme (he/she sleeps)	loro dormono (they sleep)	lui/lei ha dormito (he/she slept)	loro hanno dormito (they slept)
Imperfect Indicative		*Future*	
io dormivo (I was sleeping)	noi dormivamo (we were sleeping)	io dormirò (I will sleep)	noi dormiremo (we will sleep)
tu dormivi (you were sleeping)	voi dormivate (you were sleeping)	tu dormirai (you will sleep)	voi dormirete (you will sleep)
lui/lei dormiva (he/she was sleeping)	loro dormivano (they were sleeping)	lui/lei dormirà (he/she will sleep)	loro dormiranno (they will sleep)
Conditional			
io dormirei (I would love)	noi dormiremmo (we would love)		
tu dormiresti (you would love)	voi dormireste (you would love)		
lui/lei dormirebbe (he/she would love)	loro dormirebbero (they would love)		

3rd Conjugation: finire / to finish

Singular	Plural	Singular	Plural
Present Indicative		*Present Perfect*	
io finisco (I finish)	noi finiamo (we finish)	io ho finito (I finished)	noi abbiamo finito (we finished)
tu finisci (you finish)	voi finite (you finish)	tu hai finito (you finished)	voi avete finito (you finished)
lui/lei finisce (he/she finishes)	loro finiscono (they finish)	lui/lei ha finito (he/she finished)	loro hanno finito (they finished)
Imperfect Indicative		*Future*	
io finivo (I was finishing)	noi finivamo (we were finishing)	io finirò (I will finish)	noi finiremo (we will finish)
tu finivi (you were finishing)	voi finivate (you were finishing)	tu finirai (you will finish)	voi finirete (you will sleep)
lui/lei finiva (he/she was finishing)	loro finivano (they were finishing)	lui/lei finirà (he/she will finish)	loro finiranno (they will finish)
Conditional			
io finirei (I would finish)	noi finiremmo (we would finish)		
tu finiresti (you would finish)	voi finireste (you would finish)		
lui/lei finirebbe (he/she would finish)	loro finirebbero (they would finish)		

Note: Some verbs are conjugated with essere in the present perfect. One example will suffice:

andare / to go

Singular		Plural	
io sono andato/andata	I have gone	noi siamo andati/andate	we have gone
tu sei andato/andata	you have gone	voi siete andati/andate	you have gone
lui/lei è andato/andata	he/she has gone	loro sono andati/andate	they have gone

Irregular Verbs (Puzzles 57, 58, 81, 82)

avere / to have

Present Indicative
(io) ho, (tu) hai, (lui/lei) ha, (noi) abbiamo, (voi) avete, (loro) hanno

Present Perfect
(io) ho avuto, (tu) hai avuto, (lui/lei) ha avuto, (noi) abbiamo avuto, (voi) avete avuto, (loro) hanno avuto

Imperfect Indicative
(io) avevo, (tu) avevi, (lui/lei) aveva, (noi) avevamo, (voi) avevate, (loro) avevano

Future
(io) avrò, (tu) avrai, (lui/lei) avrà, (noi) avremo, (voi) avrete, (loro) avranno

Conditional
(io) avrei, (tu) avresti, (lui/lei) avrebbe, (noi) avremmo, (voi) avrete, (loro) avrebbero

bere / to drink

Present Indicative
(io) bevo, (tu) bevi, (lui/lei) beve, (noi) beviamo, (voi) bevete, (loro) bevono

Present Perfect
(io) ho bevuto, (tu) hai bevuto, (lui/lei) ha bevuto, (noi) abbiamo bevuto, (voi) avete bevuto, (loro) hanno bevuto

Imperfect Indicative
(io) bevevo, (tu) bevevi, (lui/lei) beveva, (noi) bevevamo, (voi) bevevate, (loro) bevevano

Future
(io) berrò, (tu) berrai, (lui/lei) berrà, (noi) berremo, (voi) berrete, (loro) berranno

Conditional
(io) berrei, (tu) berresti, (lui/lei) berrebbe, (noi) berremmo, (voi) berreste, (loro) berrebbero

dire / to say

Present Indicative
(io) dico, (tu) dici, (lui/lei) dice, (noi) diciamo, (voi) dite, (loro) dicono

Present Perfect
(io) ho detto, (tu) hai detto, (lui/lei) ha detto, (noi) abbiamo detto,
(voi) avete detto, (loro) hanno detto

Imperfect Indicative
(io) dicevo, (tu) dicevi, (lui/lei) diceva, (noi) dicevamo, (voi) dicevate,
(loro) dicevano

Future
(io) dirò, (tu) dirai, (lui/lei) dirà, (noi) diremo, (voi) direte, (loro) diranno

Conditional
(io) direi, (tu) diresti, (lui/lei) direbbe, (noi) diremmo, (voi) direste,
(loro) direbbero

dovere / to have to

Present Indicative
(io) devo, (tu) devi, (lui/lei) deve, (noi) dobbiamo, (voi) dovete, (loro) devono

Present Perfect
(io) ho dovuto, (tu) hai dovuto, (lui/lei) ha dovuto, (noi) abbiamo dovuto,
(voi) avete dovuto, (loro) hanno dovuto

Imperfect Indicative
(io) dovevo, (tu) dovevi, (lui/lei) doveva, (noi) dovevamo, (voi) dovevate,
(loro) dovevano

Future
(io) dovrò, (tu) dovrai, (lui/lei) dovrà, (noi) dovremo, (voi) dovrete,
(loro) dovranno

Conditional
(io) dovrei, (tu) dovresti, (lui/lei) dovrebbe, (noi) dovremmo, (voi) dovreste,
(loro) dovrebbero

essere / to be

Present Indicative
(io) sono, (tu) sei, (lui/lei) è, (noi) siamo, (voi) siete, (loro) sono

Present Perfect
(io) sono stato/stata, (tu) sei stato/stata, (lui/lei) è stato/stata,
(noi) siamo stati/state, (voi) siete stati/state, (loro) sono stati/state

Imperfect Indicative
(io) ero, (tu) eri, (lui/lei) era, (noi) eravamo, (voi) eravate, (loro) erano

Future
(io) sarò, (tu) sarai, (lui/lei) sarà, (noi) saremo, (voi) sarete, (loro) saranno

Conditional
(io) sarei, (tu) saresti, (lui/lei) sarebbe, (noi) saremmo, (voi) sareste,
(loro) sarebbero

fare / to do, to make

Present Indicative
(io) faccio, (tu) fai, (lui/lei) fa, (noi) facciamo, (voi) fate, (loro) fanno

Present Perfect
(io) ho fatto, (tu) hai fatto, (lui/lei) ha fatto, (noi) abbiamo fatto,
(voi) avete fatto, (loro) hanno fatto

Imperfect Indicative
(io) facevo, (tu) facevi, (lui/lei) faceva, (noi) facevamo, (voi) facevate,
(loro) facevano

Future
(io) farò, (tu) farai, (lui/lei) farà, (noi) faremo, (voi) farete, (loro) faranno

Conditional
(io) farei, (tu) faresti, (lui/lei) farebbe, (noi) faremmo, (voi) fareste,
(loro) farebbero

potere / to be able to (can)

Present Indicative
(io) posso, (tu) puoi, (lui/lei) può, (noi) possiamo, (voi) potete, (loro) possono

Present Perfect
(io) ho potuto, (tu) hai potuto, (lui/lei) ha potuto, (noi) abbiamo potuto, (voi) avete potuto, (loro) hanno potuto

Imperfect Indicative
(io) potevo, (tu) potevi, (lui/lei) poteva, (noi) potevamo, (voi) potevate, (loro) potevano

Future
(io) potrò, (tu) potrai, (lui/lei) potrà, (noi) potremo, (voi) potrete, (loro) potranno

Conditional
(io) potrei, (tu) potresti, (lui/lei) potrebbe, (noi) potremmo, (voi) potreste, (loro) potrebbero

prendere / to take

Present Indicative
(io) prendo, (tu) prendi, (lui/lei) prende, (noi) prendiamo, (voi) prendete, (loro) prendono

Present Perfect
(io) ho preso, (tu) hai preso, (lui/lei) ha preso, (noi) abbiamo preso, (voi) avete preso, (loro) hanno preso

Imperfect Indicative
(io) prendevo, (tu) prendevi, (lui/lei) prendeva, (noi) prendevamo, (voi) prendevate, (loro) prendevano

Future
(io) prenderò, (tu) prenderai, (lui/lei) prenderà, (noi) prenderemo, (voi) prenderete, (loro) prenderanno

Conditional
(io) prenderei, (tu) prenderesti, (lui/lei) prenderebbe, (noi) prenderemmo, (voi) prendereste, (loro) prenderebbero

sapere / to know

Present Indicative
(io) so, (tu) sai, (lui/lei) sa, (noi) sappiamo, (voi) sapete, (loro) sanno

Present Perfect
(io) ho saputo, (tu) hai saputo, (lui/lei) ha saputo, (noi) abbiamo saputo, (voi) avete saputo, (loro) hanno saputo

Imperfect Indicative
(io) sapevo, (tu) sapevi, (lui/lei) sapeva, (noi) sapevamo, (voi) sapevate, (loro) sapevano

Future
(io) saprò, (tu) saprai, (lui/lei) saprà, (noi) sapremo, (voi) saprete, (loro) sapranno

Conditional
(io) saprei, (tu) sapresti, (lui/lei) saprebbe, (noi) sapremmo, (voi) sapreste, (loro) saprebbero

scrivere / to write

Present Indicative
(io) scrivo, (tu) scrivi, (lui/lei) scrive, (noi) scriviamo, (voi) scrivete, (loro) scrivono

Present Perfect
(io) ho scritto, (tu) hai scritto, (lui/lei) ha scritto, (noi) abbiamo scritto, (voi) avete scritto, (loro) hanno scritto

Imperfect Indicative
(io) scrivevo, (tu) scrivevi, (lui/lei) scriveva, (noi) scrivevamo, (voi) scrivevate, (loro) scrivevano

Future
(io) scriverò, (tu) scriverai, (lui/lei) scriverà, (noi) scriveremo, (voi) scriverete, (loro) scriveranno

Conditional
(io) scriverei, (tu) scriveresti, (lui/lei) scriverebbe, (noi) scriveremmo, (voi) scrivereste, (loro) scriverebbero

uscire / to go out

Present Indicative
(io) esco, (tu) esci, (lui/lei) esce, (noi) usciamo, (voi) uscite, (loro) escono

Present Perfect
(io) sono uscito/uscita, (tu) sei uscito/uscita, (lui/lei) è uscito/uscita,
(noi) siamo usciti/uscite, (voi) siete usciti/uscite, (loro) sono usciti/uscite

Imperfect Indicative
(io) uscivo, (tu) uscivi, (lui/lei) usciva, (noi) uscivamo, (voi) uscivate,
(loro) uscivano

Future
(io) uscirò, (tu) uscirai, (lui/lei) uscirà, (noi) usciremo, (voi) uscirete,
(loro) usciranno

Conditional
(io) uscirei, (tu) usciresti, (lui/lei) uscirebbe, (noi) usciremmo, (voi) uscireste,
(loro) uscirebbero

volere / to want

Present Indicative
(io) voglio, (tu) vuoi, (lui/lei) vuole, (noi) vogliamo, (voi) volete, (loro) vogliono

Present Perfect
(io) ho voluto, (tu) hai voluto, (lui/lei) ha voluto, (noi) abbiamo voluto,
(voi) avete voluto, (loro) hanno voluto

Imperfect Indicative
(io) volevo, (tu) volevi, (lui/lei) voleva, (noi) volevamo, (voi) volevate,
(loro) volevano

Future
(io) vorrò, (tu) vorrai, (lui/lei) vorrà, (noi) vorremo, (voi) vorrete,
(loro) vorranno

Conditional
(io) vorrei, (tu) vorresti, (lui/lei) vorrebbe, (noi) vorremmo, (voi) vorreste,
(loro) vorrebbero

Glossary

The words and expressions below are the ones needed to solve the puzzles. They are listed here for your convenience.

m. = masculine
f. = feminine
pl. = plural

A

a cena	at dinner
abbonato *m.*	subscriber
abete *m.*	fir tree
abile	capable
Abito in via …	I live at …
acero *m.*	maple tree
acqua	water
acqua minerale *f.*	mineral water
aggressore *m.*	attacker
al corridoio	by the aisle
al finestrino	by the window
al forno	baked
al mare	to the sea
al sugo	with sauce
albicocca *f.*	apricot
all'estero	abroad
alla griglia	grilled
alla radio	on the radio
Alla salute!	To your health!
alle nove	at nine (o'clock)
allergia *f.*	allergy
alpinismo *m.*	mountain climbing
alto	tall
altruista *m./f.*	altruist
alzeresti	you would lift
amaro	bitter
ambulanza *f.*	ambulance
amiamo	we love
amiche *f. pl.*	friends
amici *m. pl.*	friends
anatomico	anatomical
anatra *f.*	duck

andare al cinema	to go to the movies
anello *m.*	ring
antenna parabolica *f.*	dish antenna
antipasto *m.*	appetizer, starter
aquila *f.*	eagle
arancia *f.*	orange
aranciata *f.*	orangeade
arancione	orange
architetto *m.*	architect
armadio *m.*	cabinet
Arrivederci!	Good-bye!
arrostito	roasted
arrosto *m.*	roast
asciugamani *m. pl.*	towels
asciugatrice *f.*	dryer
asciutto	dry
asino *m.*	donkey
aspro	sour
assaggiare	to taste
assistente di volo *m./f.*	flight attendant
assumere	to hire
atletico	athletic
attaccapanni *m.*	clothes hanger
ausiliare medico *m.*	paramedic
autostrada *f.*	highway
avevate	you had
avreste	you would have
avuto	had
avverbi *m. pl.*	adverbs
avvocato *m.*	lawyer
azzurro	light blue

B

bagnato	wet
bagno *m.*	bathroom
banana *f.*	banana
barbiere *m.*	barber
baseball *m.*	baseball
basso	short
Basta!	Enough!
baule *m.*	trunk

125

bella *f.*	beautiful	carciofo *m.*	artichoke
ben cotto	well-done	carie *f.*	tooth decay
bene	well	carote *f., pl.*	carrots
bere	to drink	carta (telefonica) *f.*	phone card
berrebbero	they would drink	carta d'imbarco *f.*	boarding pass
bevanda analcolica *f.*	soft drink	carta di credito *f.*	credit card
bevevate	you were drinking	carte da gioco *f. pl.*	playing cards
bianco	white	cartella *f.*	file folder
biblioteca *f.*	library	castagno *m.*	chestnut tree
bicchiere *m.*	drinking glass	castoro *m.*	beaver
birra *f.*	beer	catena *f.*	chain
biscotti *m. pl.*	cookies, biscuits	cavallo *m.*	horse
bistecca *f.*	steak	cavità *f.*	cavity
bocca *f.*	mouth	cavo *m.*	cable
borsa *f.*	purse	cavolo *m.*	cabbage
bottiglia *f.*	bottle	cellulare *m.*	cellphone
bottone *m.*	button	centro *m.*	downtown,
braccio *m.*	arm		city center
budino *m.*	pudding		
bufalo *m.*	buffalo	Certo!	Certainly!
buona *(f.)*	good	cervo *m.*	deer
burro *m.*	butter	cetriolo *m.*	cucumber
		chi	who
		chiave *f.*	key
C		chiesa *f.*	church
caffè *m.*	coffee	ciambella *f.*	donut
caffettiera *f.*	coffeemaker	Ciao!	Hi!
calcio *m.*	soccer	ciclamino *m.*	cyclamen
caldo (Fa caldo)	hot (It's hot)	cicogna *f.*	stork
calendario *m.*	calendar	cigno *m.*	swan
calmo	calm	ciliege *f. pl.*	cherries
calza *f.*	stocking	ciliegio *m.*	cherry tree
calzino *m.*	sock	cintura di	
cambiarsi	to change (oneself)	sicurezza *f.*	safety belt
camera (da letto) *f.*	bedroom	cintura *f.*	belt
camera *f.*	room	cipolla *f.*	onion
cameriera *f.*	waitress	cliccare	to click on
cameriere *m.*	waiter	cofano *m.*	hood
camicetta *f.*	blouse	cognome *m.*	surname (family
camicia *f.*	shirt		name)
campeggio *m.*	camping	collana *f.*	necklace
campo *m.*	field	colomba *f.*	dove
cantate	you sing	coltello *m.*	knife
capitale *f.*	capital	comandante *m./f.*	captain
capito	understood	come	how
capolinea *m.*	bus station	comincerebbe	he/she would start
cappello *m.*	hat	comò *m.*	dresser
capra *f.*	goat	compact disc *m.*	compact disc
carattere *m.*	character	comprerei	I would buy

con noi	with us
condizioni *f. pl.*	conditions
conducente *m./f.*	driver
contabile *m./f.*	accountant
contadino *m.*	farmer
coperto (Il cielo è coperto)	overcast (The sky is overcast)
cornetto *m.*	croissant
cosa	what
cravatta *f.*	tie
creativo	creative
cucchiaio *m.*	spoon
cucina *f.*	kitchen
cuginetti *m. pl.*	little cousins
cuochi *m. pl.*	cooks

D

Da Vinci (Leonardo da Vinci)	Leonardo Da Vinci
dagli zii	at our uncles' (place)
dalia *f.*	dahlia
dama *f.*	checkers
Dante (Alighieri)	Dante Alighieri
davvero	really
decollo *m.*	take-off
dello zio	of the uncle
dentiera *f.*	denture
dentista *m./f.*	dentist
deve	he/she has to
dice	he/she says
dicevate	you were saying
digerire	to digest
diranno	they will say
direi	I would say
disoccupate *f. pl.* (disoccupato)	unemployed
dodici	twelve
dolce	sweet
dolore *m.*	pain
domani	tomorrow
donna *f.*	woman
dopo domani	after tomorrow
dorme	he/she sleeps
dormirò	I will sleep
dormono	they sleep
dove	where
duro	hard

E

edificio *m.*	building
egoista *m./f.*	egoist
elefante *m.*	elephant
elegante *(f.)*	elegant
elenco (telefonico) *m.*	phone book
elettricista *m./f.*	electrician
email *f.*	e-mail
entrata *f.*	entrance
erano	they were
erbaccia *f.*	weed
eri	you were
escono	they go out
esercitarsi	to exercise
essere umano *m.*	human being

F

fabbrica *f.*	factory
facevamo	we were doing
fagioli *m. pl.*	beans
falchi *m. pl.*	falcons
falegname *m.*	carpenter
fanno	they do
fantasia *f.*	creative imagination
fare delle spese	to shop
fare il biglietto	to purchase a ticket
fare jogging	to jog
fare una passeggiata	to go for a walk
faremo	we will do
fari *m. pl.*	headlights
fattoria *f.*	farm
febbre *f.*	fever
Fellini (Federico Fellini)	Federico Fellini
fermata *f.*	stop
ferrovia *f.*	railroad
finestra *f.*	window
finirei	I would finish
finirò	I will finish
finiscono	they finish
finito	finished
finivo	I was finishing
fiori *m. pl.*	flowers
Firenze	Florence
foglia *f.*	leaf
football americano *m.*	football
forbici *f. pl.*	scissors
forchetta *f.*	fork

formaggio *m.*	cheese
forte	strong
fotocamera *f.*	photo camera
fragole *f. pl.*	strawberries
fratello *m.*	brother
freddo (Fa freddo)	cold (It's cold)
freno *m.*	brake
frutti di mare *m. pl.*	seafood
fungo *m.*	mushroom
futuro *m.*	future

G

gabbiano *m.*	seagull
gallina *f.*	hen
gallo *m.*	rooster
gamba *f.*	leg
gamberi *m. pl.*	shrimp
garage *m.*	garage
garofano *m.*	carnation
gelato *m.*	ice cream
generoso	generous
gente *f.*	people
gentile	gentle, kind
geranio *m.*	geranium
ghiaccio *m.*	ice
giacca *f.*	jacket
giallo	yellow
giardino *m.*	garden
ginnastica *f.*	gymnastics
gioia *f.*	joy
giornali *m. pl.*	newspapers
giraffa *f.*	giraffe
giramento di testa *m.*	dizziness
golf *m.*	golf
gomma *f.*	rubber
gonna *f.*	skirt
gorilla *m.*	gorilla
gracile	slender
granturco *m.*	corn
grappetta *f.*	paper clip
grasso	fat
Grazie!	Thank you!
greci *m. pl.*	Greeks
grosso	huge
guanto *m.*	glove
guarderà	he/she will look
guarderò	I will watch

H

hamburger *m.*	hamburger
hockey *m.*	hockey

I

idraulico *m.*	plumber
ieri	yesterday
imperfetto *m.*	imperfect
impiegato *m.*	office worker
impiego *m.*	job
impiombatura *f.*	filling
Impossibile!	Impossible!
in inverno	in the winter
in montagna	in the mountains
inchiesta *f.*	inquiry
incrocio *m.*	intersection
indicativo *m.*	indicative
infermiera *f.*	nurse
influenza *f.*	flu
iniezione *f.*	needle
insalata di riso *f.*	rice salad
interruttore *m.*	switch
interurbana *f.*	long-distance call
irregolari *m. pl.*	irregular

L

l'una e cinque	five past one
l'una e mezzo	half past one
labbra *f. pl.* (il labbro)	lips
ladro *m.*	thief
lampada *f.*	lamp
lampadina *f.*	light bulb
lamponi *m. pl.*	raspberries
latte *m.*	milk
lattuga *f.*	lettuce
lavastoviglie *f.*	dishwasher
lavatrice *f.*	washer
laverete	you will wash
lavorare	to work
le dieci del mattino	ten in the morning
le due e un quarto	a quarter past two
le quattordici	two in the afternoon
le ventidue	ten at night
leone *m.*	lion
letto *m.*	bed
lettura *f.*	reading
licenziare	to fire (from a job)
limonata *f.*	lemonade

liscio	smooth
loro	their
luci *f. pl.*	lights
luoghi *m. pl.*	places
M	
madre *f.*	mother
Magari!	I wish!
maglia *f.*	sweater
magro	thin, skinny
mal di testa *m.*	headache
mancia *f.*	tip
mangerei	I would eat
mangiare	to eat
mangiato	eaten
mangiava	he was eating
mani *f. pl.*	hands
mano *f.*	hand
Manzoni (Alessandro Manzoni)	Alessandro Manzoni
marciapiede *m.*	sidewalk
margherite *f. pl.*	daisies
marmellata *f.*	marmalade
marrone	brown
maternità *f.*	maternity ward
matita *f.*	pencil
maturo	ripe
medico *m.*	doctor
mela *f.*	apple
melo *m.*	apple tree
menu *m.*	menu
mettersi	to put on
mezzanotte *f.*	midnight
mezzogiorno *m.*	noon
Mi chiamo ...	My name is ...
Michelangelo (Michelangelo Buonarroti)	Michelangelo
mille	one thousand
mio	my
molle	soft
montone *m.*	ram
mouse *m.*	computer mouse
mucca *f.*	cow
mughetto *m.*	lily of the valley
muscoloso	muscular
museo *m.*	museum
musicista *m./f.*	musician

N	
naso *m.*	nose
nausea *f.*	nausea
navigare	to navigate
negozio *m.*	store
nel cassetto	in the drawer
nero	black
nervoso	nervous
nevica	it's snowing
nome *m.*	given (first) name
Non ci credo!	I don't believe it!
nonni *m. pl.*	grandparents
nostro	our
nuotare	to swim
nuvoloso (È nuvoloso)	cloudy (It's cloudy)
O	
occhio *m.*	eye
oggi	today
ondulato	wavy
operazione *f.*	operation
orario *m.*	schedule
orecchino *m.*	earring
orecchio *m.*	ear
orologio *m.*	clock, watch
orso *m.*	bear
ospedale *m.*	hospital
ossuto	bony
ottanta	eighty
P	
pacco *m.*	package
padre *m.*	father
palestra *f.*	gymnasium
pallacanestro *f.*	basketball
pane *m.*	bread
panini *m. pl.*	buns
pansè *f.*	pansy
pantaloni *m. pl.*	pants
papà *m.*	dad
parabolica (antenna parabolica) *f.*	satellite dish
parabrezza *m.*	windshield
paraurti *m.*	bumper
parchimetro *m.*	parking meter
parco *m.*	park
parlato	spoken

parli	you speak	portatile *m.*	laptop
parole crociate *f. pl.*	crosswords	porterebbe	he/she would bring
parrucchiere *m.*	hairdresser	porteremo	we will bring
participi *m. pl.*	participles	porzione *f.*	serving
partireste	you would leave	possessivo	possessive
passatempo *m.*	hobby	posso	I can
patata *f.*	potato	poteva	he/she could
patate fritte *f. pl.*	fried potatoes	praticare gli sport	to practice sports
patatine fritte *f. pl.*	fries	precedenza *f.*	yield
pausa del caffè *f.*	coffee-break	preferirebbero	they would prefer
pavimento *m.*	floor	preferisco	I prefer
pecora *f.*	sheep	Prego!	You're welcome!
pendolare *m./f.*	commuter	prendere	to have (something)
penna *f.*	pen	prenotazione *f.*	reservation
pensione *f.*	pension, bed-and-breakfast	preposizione *f.*	preposition
		presente *m.*	present
Per favore!	Please!	preso	taken
per me	for me	primo	first
pera *f.*	pear	professore *m.*	professor
perché	why	programma *m.*	program
periferia *f.*	suburbs	pronto soccorso *m.*	emergency ward
pero *m.*	pear tree	Pronto!	Hello (on the phone)!
persone *f. pl.*	persons		
pesca *f.*	peach	prosciutto cotto *m.*	cooked ham
Piacere!	A pleasure!	provarsi	to try on
piani *m. pl.*	floors	proveremmo	we would try
piano *m.*	floor	prugna *f.*	plum
piatto *m.*	plate	punta (l'ora di punta)	rush hour
piazze *f. pl.*	town squares	puntate (programma a puntate)	serial program
piccante	spicy		
piccione *m.*	pigeon	punto metallico *m.*	staple
piede *m.*	foot	puzzle *m.*	jigsaw puzzle
pilota *m.*	pilot		
pinguino *m.*	penguin	**Q**	
piove	it's raining	quadro *m.*	painting
piscine *f.*	pool	quale	which
pista di sci *f.*	ski slope	quando	when
plurale *m.*	plural	quanto	how much
plurali *m. pl.*	plurals	quello	that
pneumatico *m.*	tire	quercia *f.*	oak tree
poliziotto *m.*	policeman	questo	this
poltrona *f.*	armchair	quieto	quiet
pomodoro *m.*	tomato	quindicesimo	fifteenth
pompiere *m.*	fireman		
ponte *m.*	bridge	**R**	
popolo *m.*	populace	radice *f.*	root
porta *f.*	door	radio *f.*	radio, radios
portafoglio *m.*	wallet	raffreddore *m.*	common cold

ragazze *f. pl.*	girls
ragazzi *m. pl.*	boys
ramo *m.*	branch
rete *f.*	network
rianimazione (sala di rianimazione) *f.*	intensive care ward
ricevete	you receive
riescono	they succeed
riga *f.*	ruler
rione *m.*	district
ristorante *m.*	restaurant
Roma	Rome
rosa	pink
Rossini (Gioacchino Rossini)	Gioacchino Rossini
rosso	red
rotondo	round
rozzo	rough, uncouth
rubinetto *m.*	faucet

S

sala da pranzo	dining room
salame *m.*	salami
salato	salty
salmone *m.*	salmon
salotto *m.*	living room
sandalo *m.*	sandal
sapete	they know
saprete	you will know
saputo	known
saranno	they will be
sardine *f. pl.*	sardines
sarto *m.*	tailor
scacchi *m. pl.*	chess
scaffale *m.*	bookcase
scale *f. pl.*	stairs
scarpa *f.*	shoe
schermo *m.*	screen
sci *m.*	skiing
sciarpa *f.*	scarf
scimmia *f.*	monkey
scritto	written
scrivania *f.*	desk
scuola *f.*	school
Scusi!	Excuse me!
sedano *m.*	celery
sedia *f.*	chair
semaforo *m.*	traffic lights

semenza *f.*	seed(s)
sempre	always
server *m.*	server
servire	to serve
sete *f.*	thirst
settanta	seventy
siete	you are
simpatica *(f.)*	nice
simpatico *(m.)*	nice
sincero	sincere
sindacato *m.*	labor union
sitcom *f.*	sitcom
sito (web) *m.*	website
smalto *m.*	nail polish
sofà *m.*	couch, sofa
soffitta *f.*	attic
soffitto *m.*	ceiling
soldi *m. pl.*	money
sole (C'è il sole)	sun (It's sunny)
sorella *f.*	sister
sorpassare	to pass
sotto la sedia	under the chair
sottopassaggio *m.*	underpass
spaghetti *m. pl.*	spaghetti
spilla *f.*	broach
spogliarsi	to get undressed
stadio *m.*	stadium
stampante *f.*	printer
starnutire	to sneeze
stato	been
stazione ferroviaria *f.*	train station
stelo *m.*	stem
stereo *m.*	stereo
stivale *m.*	boot
strada *f.*	street
stupidità *f.*	stupidity
sul tavolo	on the table
suo	his/her/your
suola *f.*	sole

T

tacchino *m.*	turkey
tacco *m.*	heel
tagliare	to cut
tagliarsi i capelli	to cut one's hair
tastiera *f.*	keyboard
tavola *f.*	table
tazza *f.*	cup

teiera *f.*	teapot	userai	you will use
telecomando *m.*	remote control	uva *f.*	grapes
telecomunicazioni *f. pl.*	communications		
		V	
telefonico (numero telefonico)	phone number	Va bene!	OK!
		vacanze *f. pl.*	vacations
telefonino *m.*	cellphone	vedono	they see
televisore *m.*	television set	vende	he/she sells
tennis *m.*	tennis	venderà	he/she will sell
testa *f.*	head	venderemmo	we would sell
topo *m.*	mouse	vendevano	they were selling
Tornatore (Giuseppe Tornatore)	Giuseppe Tornatore	vento (Tira vento)	wind (It's windy)
		ventunesimo	twenty-first
torre *f.*	tower	verde	green
torta *f.*	cake	Verdi (Giuseppe Verdi)	Giuseppe Verdi
tossire	to cough		
tovaglia *f.*	tablecloth	versare	to pour
tramezzino *m.*	flat sandwich	vestirsi	to get dressed
trecento	three hundred	vestito *m.*	dress
tribunale *m.*	courthouse	vicino	nearby
tristezza *f.*	sadness	vicolo *m.*	alley
trombone *m.*	daffodil	videoregistratore *m.*	video recorder
trucco *m.*	make-up	vino *m.*	wine
tulipani *m. pl.*	tulips	viola	purple
tuo	your	viola *f.*	violet
		volante *m.*	steering wheel
U		vomitare	to vomit
ufficio *m.*	office	vorremmo	we would want
ulivo *m.*	olive tree	vostro	your
un milione	one million		
un terzo	one third	**W, Z**	
università *f.*	university	würstel *m.*	hot dog
uomini *m. pl.*	men	zia *f.*	aunt
uomo *m.*	man	zio *m.*	uncle
uova *f. pl.* (uovo *m.*)	eggs	zoo *m.*	zoo

Break the Foreign Language Barrier with Barron's Language Series!

VERB SERIES

Over 300 of the most frequently used verbs in six foreign languages are presented in handy reference guides. Each guide displays fully conjugated verbs in all their forms, arranged alphabetically for quick and easy location. The idioms and expressions related to each verb are listed at the bottom of each page. A helpful index listing approximately 1000 additional verbs is included in each book. Here is wonderful review material for students, travelers, and business people.

Each book: $5.95–$7.95, Can.$7.95–$11.50
French Verbs
German Verbs
Italian Verbs
Spanish Verbs

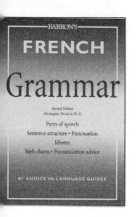

GRAMMAR SERIES

A comprehensive study of the elements of grammar and usage in six prominent languages makes these handy reference guides ideal for anyone just beginning a language study and those who wish to review what they've already learned. Parts of speech, sentence structure, lists of synonyms and antonyms, idiomatic phrases, days, dates, numbers, and much more are all reviewed. Also featured are guides to word pronunciation and sentence punctuation in each of the languages.

French Grammar, $5.95, Can.$8.50
German Grammar, $7.95, Can.$11.50
Italian Grammar, $6.95, Can.$8.95
Japanese Grammar, $6.95, Can.$8.95
Russian Grammar, $6.95, Can.$8.95
Spanish Grammar, $5.95, Can.$8.50

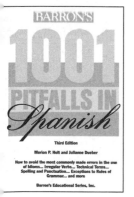

1001 PITFALLS SERIES

An all-inclusive series that eliminates frustration by effectively helping the beginning or advanced student through the most troublesome aspects of learning a foreign language. Overcome the difficult details of grammar, usage and style in three important European languages, with consistent use of these guides. Ideal for both individual and classroom use as a supplement to regular textbooks.

1001 Pitfalls in French, 3rd, $13.95, Can.$19.95

1001 Pitfalls in German, 3rd, $12.95, Can.$18.95

1001 Pitfalls in Spanish, 3rd, $10.95, Can.$14.50

Books may be purchased at your bookstore, or by mail from Barron's. Enclose check or money order for the total amount plus sales tax where applicable and 18% for postage and handling charge (minimum charge $5.95, Canada $4.00). New York, New Jersey, Michigan, and California residents add sales tax. Prices subject to change without notice.
ISBN PREFIX 0-8120 Can$ = Price in Canadian Dollars

Barron's Educational Series, Inc.
250 Wireless Blvd., Hauppauge, NY 11788
In Canada: Georgetown Book Warehouse
34 Armstrong Ave., Georgetown, Ontario L7G 4R9

R 10/05